GATHERED IN
THE WORD

GATHERED IN THE WORD

Norvene Vest

UPPER
ROOM BOOKS
NASHVILLE

Gathered in the Word: Praying the Scripture in Small Groups
© 1996 by Norvene Vest
All rights reserved.

Art direction: Michele Wetherbee
Design: Laura Beers
Photograph: © 1996 Jennifer Baumann/Graphistock
Interior design: C. Sutherland Book Designs

Library of Congress Cataloging-in-Publication Data

Vest, Norvene.
    Gathered in the Word : praying the Scripture in small groups / Novene Vest.
        p. cm.
    Includes bibliographical references.
    ISBN 0-8358-0806-8 (paper)
    1. Bible—Devotional use. 2. Prayer groups—Christianity.
I. Title.
BS617.8.V48   1997
    220' .07—dc20   96-43231
                                    CIP

Printed in the United States of America

The Holy Spirit is moving strongly in the world today to bring about a renewal in the church through a return to vital elements of Christian tradition. This book is the fruit of the Spirit's touch upon many hearts, and I am grateful to all who, being faithful to their individual call, are joining in the rebirth of *lectio divina.*

In particular, I express my thanks to the many "pilgrims" who have traveled with my husband, Douglas, and me to England and Wales on our Benedictine Fortnights and who have been unanimous in their praise of group *lectio* as the heartbeat of our pilgrimages. It is through their encouragement that this book was written.

TABLE OF CONTENTS

Introduction

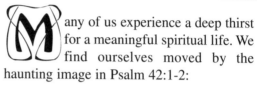

Many of us experience a deep thirst for a meaningful spiritual life. We find ourselves moved by the haunting image in Psalm 42:1-2:

> As a deer longs for flowing streams, so my soul longs for you, O God. My soul thirsts for God, for the living God.

Our souls thirst, our hearts long for the touch of the living God. We feel the need for genuine spiritual refreshment as we wander through an environment all too often parched and dry. We long for an affirming relationship with God that will make a difference in how we experience daily life. We eagerly set out on the inviting journey of spiritual growth, seeking deeper relationship with God's very self.

We may begin such a journey by doing some reading, engaging in some worship, trying to live attuned to God's presence. Yet before we get very far, we discover that we cannot go it alone. We need help, advice, and guidance. We need the wisdom that comes from others who are well-advanced in this spiritual journey. Yet most of us do not have many such souls in our immediate surround-

9

ings, and we may begin to feel discouraged and abandoned. Sometimes it seems that our search for spiritual growth serves more to emphasize our dryness, rather than to lead us to waters of refreshing coolness.

In particular, we may be disappointed by the Bible, a foundational resource that our spiritual ancestors seem to have found fruitful. Turning to the holy scriptures of the Judeo-Christian tradition, we occasionally may find ourselves bewildered, disappointed, or sometimes downright alienated by what appears to be an experience so far removed from our own that we cannot find any way to unlock its value. Is the living, compassionate God revealed in scripture in a way that offers us guidance and comfort in our daily living? This book affirms that it is indeed! There is even a time-honored method of reading the Bible that teaches us to encounter God specifically in that way. This book shows how our scriptures can genuinely and consistently aid our spiritual growth rather than being another dry well.

The simple process of Bible reflection presented here is intended specifically for spiritual nourishment. We often think of reading the Bible as a process of *study*. But there is a way of reading the Bible *devotionally* to satisfy spiritual thirst. Christians have long known a means of turning to scripture that transcends any time and culture-specific references, reaching into the reader's present experience to facilitate spiritual growth.[1] Yet this older process has been set aside in the "rational" centuries from the Reformation (sixteenth century) through the Enlightenment (eighteenth century); that is, the time when a definitive split between sacred and secular emerged through dramatic changes in philosophy and the arts, politics and economics, trade and daily life. In general, our post-Enlightenment twentieth century tends to emphasize a historical and analytical approach toward any text. Systematic analysis of the scripture has yielded many valuable insights about events at the time of writing, the relationship between various editors, and the like. But these details have tended to overwhelm a more devotional method of presence to the scripture. While this approach has achieved many gains, it has neglected an older tradition that viewed the Bible as an aid to the spiritual life rather than chiefly a source of data or information!

It is now difficult for us to imagine what a devotional approach to the Bible might mean, much less how to go about it. Yet the ancient Christian art of Bible reading for spiritual growth has never been totally lost, and today it is gradually reemerging in several radically different Christian settings—from monastic communities in the United States to recently evangelized African Christians. This book offers a means of Bible reading available to all for spiritual growth.

The ancient Christian tongue twister name for the simple process on which we base our method is *lectio divina* (pronounced lex-ee-oh dih-vee-nuh). This Latin phrase literally translates into English as "divine reading" and refers primarily to the reading of sacred scriptures as practiced by the early Christian fathers and mothers. In Latin as in English, the adjective "divine" refers both to the material being read (the divine word) and the method of reading (an inspired approach). The Latin also carries a tradition of meaning that is vaster than the literal English translation suggests. Therefore, we continue to use the Latin phrase and usually shorten it simply to *lectio*.

Historically, both individuals and groups use *lectio* with much variation in actual practice. It focuses on the good word of God as revealed in divine scriptures, although it can be practiced on other readings of spiritual depth and on events drawn from daily life also. *Lectio* looks to the Bible as the word of God, a privileged text from which Christians receive continued nourishment. Yet *lectio* is not Bible *study*, for it involves neither an analysis of a scripture passage nor an emphasis on text information. Scripture study is an essential supplement to ongoing *lectio* but is not directly involved in this process. Above all, *lectio* is undertaken in the conviction that God's word is meant to be a "good" word; that is, something carrying God's own life in a way that benefits the one who receives it faithfully. *Lectio* turns to the scripture for nurture, comfort, and refreshment. *Lectio* is an encounter with the living God; it is prayer.

Lectio is a way of deep prayer, of encounter with God. Yet this mode of deep prayer differs from much modern practice. It involves reason and discursive thought, an inner exploration of meaning. It connects daily prayer both with the credal truths of the Christian tradition and with life's current issues. *Lectio* fully engages the mind and the body as active partners in spiritual nourishment. *Lectio* has both an active mode and a receptive mode; both are essential to its practice. For example, the meditative *lectio* phrase is not the same as a mantra, which is intended to quiet mental thought in order to deepen spiritual centering. On the contrary, in *lectio* we use the gifted phrase as a means of interacting directly with the actual situations of life, evoking new images and possibilities that empower us to live in congruence with our faith. The *lectio* phrase is the fruitful word of God in the sense that Isaiah intends it:

> For as the rain and snow come down from heaven, and do not return there until they have watered the earth, making it bring forth and sprout, giving seed to the sower and bread to the eater, so shall my word be that goes out from my mouth; it shall not return to me empty, but it shall accomplish that which I purpose and succeed in the thing for which I sent it.
>
> —Isaiah 55:10-11

The Group Approach to *Lectio* Practice

As used here, *lectio* is a process of group Bible reflection. This book presents a particular frame for the ancient art of Bible reading for spiritual growth—that of a group setting and a careful sequence of simple steps. *Lectio* in a group is a powerful means of invoking the Holy Spirit to support the spiritual formation of all. However, at times every reader may wish to practice *lectio* privately. The appendix suggests a method of using *lectio* for individual use as a supplement to the group practice.

The basic process for group *lectio* is roughly this: The leader reads a short passage from scripture. As the leader reads the passage again, the members listen attentively for a particular word or phrase that seems to be given to each. Then each simply speaks aloud the word received. Another member reads the same passage again, and in silence the group members ponder how the passage seems to touch their lives. Then, each member briefly speaks aloud his or her sense of being touched. Finally the same passage is read yet again, and in silence the group members reflect on a possible invitation found in the passage to do or be something in the next few days. Each speaks of his or her own invitation, and the person on the left prays for the empowerment to follow through on the invitation.

This process of group *lectio* involves a communal expression of the deep personal intimacy with God, which is at the heart of Christian faith. By and large, those of us who experience such intimacy seldom express it, much less in a group setting. We think of intimacy with God as being so personal that it often seems "indecent" to share. Certainly such faith sharing involves some risk, but this sharing is never forced. On the contrary, any verbal contribution is regarded as a gift to the group, never a demand from the group. Gradually as the group experiences the beauty of the inner life of Christ's appearing so powerfully in the context of each broken and incomplete human life, a natural and deepened reverence grows for one another. Mutual sharing about intimate experience of God— when offered freely and not demanded—enables us all to become more fully who we are. Our reverence for Christ's life in one another is bound to overflow to a new perspective even for our own embraced life situation!

We might well inquire whether we can do this effectively without some sort of professional leadership. Perhaps we worry that any meaningful group interaction with scripture needs a facilitator who is knowledgeable about scripture. Maybe we occasionally have attended "self-led" groups that seemed merely to be a pooling of ignorance or to offer a forum for sustained harangue from a single—if well-meaning—point of view. We may think that any reading of the Bible inevitably needs to teach objective and dogmatic truths of the gospel, which requires formal leadership.

Lectio does involve discipline. And one primary element of its discipline is context: It takes place with (outside) access to and study of objective information about the whole scripture and through ongoing participation in a Christian community that emphasizes foundational faith principles. But *lectio* is *not* primarily a process of knowledge acquisition (though it thrives on a growing body of careful study about scripture); it is not about mastery of truth. Instead, *lectio* is primarily a process of encounter; it is about surrender to Truth. It is a seeking of God and God's own word within the scripture. In this sense (of present and living encounter with a transforming God), there are no experts; there is no end to knowledge. As Psalm 139 suggests to us:

> How weighty to me are your thoughts, O God! How vast is the sum of them! I try to count them—they are more than the sand; I come to the end—I am still with you.
>
> —Psalm 139: 17-18

Formal or professional leadership is unnecessary for *lectio*. Effective *lectio* stems principally from silent attentiveness to the word of scripture in relation to the specifics of each individual life. Effective *lectio* emphasizes openness to personal encounter at the unique intersection of life and scripture. The primary data needed for *lectio* is the person's willingness to be open to God in her or her own life; the primary disposition needed for *lectio* is willingness to offer this life data to the presence and personal "word" of God heard by each within today's scripture.

Lectio's design facilitates an encounter with the living God in such a way that we gradually are transformed into Christ's own likeness. It is intended to enable us to release the barriers and blind spots that separate us from God and prevent us from becoming the person God continually calls each of us to be. It is meant to empower us to reconcile the world to God in Christ, becoming peacemakers and agents of justice in every arena of our lives. Many of us have no idea how to grow into the likeness of Christ; we have no conception of any means that might assist us to unfold in the spiritual growth promised to us in baptism. We have not experienced reading the Bible as a powerful aid to personal spiritual transformation. *Lectio enables this change*. It is a potent instrument, both in acknowledging our limitations and in enabling us to transcend them in Christ. It helps us become the children of God we long to be. It slakes our thirst for God in the flowing streams of scripture given to us for that purpose.

The Book's Content

This book is designed as a guide—a practical vehicle that shows how small Christian groups can meet with *lectio* practice at their center. The participants might be members of a parish or a congregation;

they might be oblates in a monastic community or groups formed ad hoc by Christians sharing work who desire to meet together with Christ at the center. Group members provide support and strength, while requiring accountability of one another.

The chapters are designed to help groups begin and continue successful *lectio* practice together. They anticipate questions that might arise and offer helpful supplemental information. Chapter 1 sets forth the *lectio* process as offered here for group use. First, it describes the process. Then it gives an example of an imaginary group experience as it might actually happen. (We follow this same imaginary sample group throughout the book.) Chapter 1 closes with a summary chart for quick reference.

Chapters 2, 3, and 4 discuss three different aspects of *lectio* practice. Chapter 2 covers the heart and rhythm of the practice, particularly in light of its underlying structure that is sometimes at variance with implicit assumptions of twentieth-century Western culture. Chapter 3 establishes basic guidelines—the nuts and bolts, as it were—of group life, showing how a group can deliberately orient itself to Christ at the center. Chapter 4 offers guidelines and sample texts that work well for group *lectio*.

Chapter 5 extends the range of *lectio* for those who are interested. It suggests that *lectio* is intended to shape the way we see and respond to the world itself, so that the "texts" we use for the (*lectio*) encounter with God may be expanded to include incidents that occur in daily life. The theory is presented, again with a sample practice and a summary chart. And chapter 6 shows how *lectio* is the rightful heritage of all Christians. The epilogue is an imaginary way of describing the personal transformation, the deepening spiritual growth in Christ that is the desire of our longing hearts.

The appendix offers guidance for individual *lectio* practice, and the footnotes and additional resources provide reading suggestions on praying scripture and group dynamics for those interested in further exploration. May God deepen your longing!

1 Praying Scripture in a Group

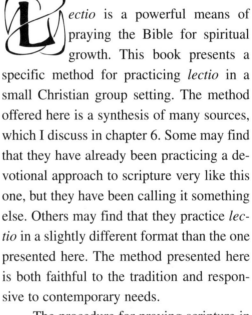

ectio is a powerful means of praying the Bible for spiritual growth. This book presents a specific method for practicing *lectio* in a small Christian group setting. The method offered here is a synthesis of many sources, which I discuss in chapter 6. Some may find that they have already been practicing a devotional approach to scripture very like this one, but they have been calling it something else. Others may find that they practice *lectio* in a slightly different format than the one presented here. The method presented here is both faithful to the tradition and responsive to contemporary needs.

The procedure for praying scripture in a group is as follows:

- After a period of preparation, the leader reads through a short passage from scripture. The leader, having asked the group members to listen attentively for a particular word or phrase that seems to be given them, reads the passage slowly a second time. After a minute of silence, the leader invites each to speak aloud the word or phrase heard and received from the passage.

- Then a member other than the leader reads the same passage aloud. In silence the group members ponder how the passage seems to touch their life. Again at the leader's invitation each briefly speaks aloud his or her sense of being touched.

- Another group member reads same passage aloud yet again. In silence the group members reflect on what the passage seems to be inviting them to do or be over the next few days. The leader invites the members to each speak aloud of their invitation.

- Finally each member prays that the person to the right will receive power to do or be what he or she feels called upon to do or be.

Let's look at this process now in more detail and with examples.

Preparation

The group members gather, sitting in a close circle. Only the leader has a Bible, and the leader has selected a passage of no more than ten verses. The leader begins by aiding the group members to become quiet and fully present, waiting in expectancy to hear and receive God in their midst. Take a few moments to relax, to release tensions and preoccupations, to become attentive to what they will hear. It helps to sit upright, alert yet comfortable; to close eyes and let attention focus on the breath; to spend a few moments in silence before anything else occurs.

Example

Three couples from Immanuel Church have been meeting once a month for dinner. They have decided they want a focus for their faith sharing, so they have committed to do *lectio* together before dinner each month. Tonight's meeting is at the home of Sharon and Charles. The other two couples (Bill and Mary, Jim and Ann) have arrived and set their potluck dishes in the kitchen. They have settled all the children in the family room with the neighbor's teenage daughter, whom they pay to supervise the children while they meet. The couples have gathered in a close circle. Sharon, the leader for the evening, convenes them. She begins by inviting everyone to "simmer down" and to mentally set aside all distractions. She encourages them to focus on their breathing, exhaling all physical tensions and enjoying a few moments of quiet.

Stage One: Hear the Word

The leader reads the selected passage aloud twice. The first hearing helps the group members orient themselves to the particular passage, listening for overall comprehension. The second reading, which follows immediately, is a bit slower. This time the leader invites members to listen attentively for a particular word or phrase that especially draws them at this moment. The word or phrase must come *from the passage itself*, and yet it need not be central to the passage.

For example, if the passage begins, "Jesus went across the lake in the boat with his disciples to pray," the word that particularly seems to call to you at the moment may be *boat*. You need not understand why; you need not explain or defend the word choice—to yourself, to the group, or to God. You simply consent to receive the word *boat*. Then you would repeat the word softly over and over to yourself in the minute of silence that follows the reading.

The group members wait to speak until the leader invites each of them to say the word or phrase aloud. No one explains or elaborates on what was heard; each person says only the word or phrase from the passage without additional comment. At any stage, a person may choose not to share but to pass—for any reason or no reason. So at this time, each member either speaks his or her word or phrase or indicates a desire to pass.

Example

Sharon has chosen a passage from the Gospel of John (1: 35-39), which she reads aloud as follows:

> The next day John again was standing with two of his disciples, and as he watched Jesus walk by, he exclaimed, "Look, here is the Lamb of God!" The two disciples heard him say

this, and they followed Jesus. When Jesus turned and saw them following, he said to them, "What are you looking for?" They said to him, "Rabbi" (which translated means Teacher), "where are you staying?" He said to them, "Come and see."

Before reading the passage again, Sharon asks the group members to listen for a word or phrase from the passage that seems to draw them or have special attraction. Then she reads the passage aloud a second time. She suggests that they repeat their word or phrase to themselves softly during a silent minute. At the end of the time, Sharon invites each to speak aloud *only* the word or phrase that was heard or to pass. Charles says, "Teacher"; Ann responds, "Followed." Mary's phrase is, "Come and see." Bill says, "What are you looking for?" Jim passes. "Come and see" also draws Sharon's attention.

Stage Two: How is my life touched?	The leader asks another person to read the passage for the second stage of the process. Choose a variety of reading voices; different voices enable us to hear different things.

Before the reading begins, the leader reminds the group members that they are to listen to the passage with the following question in mind: "How is my life touched today?" This reflection will continue in the two to three minutes of silence that follow. Normally the members will ponder this question specifically in relation to the word or phrase found during the first stage, but this is not rigid. Another word or phrase may substitute itself in this second listening.

The members may consider the question "How is my life touched today?" in one of two ways: The first way is our normal, abstract way of understanding. For example, "Considering that my life is a constellation of specific matters at the moment and that the scripture passage is also a constellation of factors, in what ways do the two seem to inform and interact with each other?"

The second way is more sensory and less abstract. You can interpret the word *touched* more literally and become receptive to a special image, sound, taste, touch, or smell that seems to be given in relation to the passage. You may not immediately understand the connection between the image that emerges and the passage itself. But again, you simply consent to accept what is given and to dwell with it and reflect on it during the silence that follows the reading.

The reader slowly reads the passage aloud only once. There is then a silence of about two minutes, during which each person reflects on how he or she senses God's touch. As before, the leader brings the silence to a close by inviting members to share *briefly* (one or two sentences) how they sense that the passage touches their lives. Members might begin with the words *I hear*, *I see*, or *I sense* and continue for one or two sentences. Choose words succinctly, without explaining or justifying what has been sensed. Anyone may choose to pass.

Example

Sharon asks Bill to read the passage, and he starts immediately. She gently interrupts him and says she would like to give a word or two of guidance before the group listens to the scripture again: "This time we are listening to the passage with the question in mind, 'How is my life touched?' We may receive a sensory touch; for example, a sight or sound may come to mind, or we may have an idea about a connection between the passage and our lives. We will take two minutes of silence for reflection after the reading." She asks Bill to begin, and he reads the passage.

After two minutes' silence, Sharon invites members to share briefly how they have sensed their lives touched, perhaps beginning with the words *I hear*, *I see*, or *I sense*. Ann begins, "I see a dusty road, very hot and dry—and in the far distance, a figure dressed in white, whom I am somehow following." Charles says, "I see Robin Williams in *Dead Poets' Society* leading his class out into the hallway to look at photos of long-dead students and urging his class to seize the day." (He gives an embarrassed laugh but does not explain further.) Mary responds, "My phrase was 'come and see,' but I didn't see anything although I seem to hear a fountain burbling. I guess I'm not doing it right." Jim breaks in, "Of course, you're doing it right; it's just a ridiculously awkward process!" Sharon smiles and signals them both to an uncomfortable silence. Bill looks up as if coming back from some faraway place and says, "That phrase just keeps haunting me—what am I seeking, what do I really want? I realize that it has been years since I even thought about such a question. Do I really want to be vice-president of my firm if it means never seeing my kids go to bed?" He shakes his head and lapses into silence.

After a period of silence, Sharon asks, "Jim, would you like to pass or share?" Jim replies, "It's obvious that all of us have to let Jesus be our leader and give us direction." After a moment, Sharon states, "My phrase was 'come and see,' and I feel there is a grown-up taking my hand (with me as a child) and walking with me to the side of a great meadow, full of beautiful yellow flowers. It is so lovely!"

Stage Three: Is there an invitation here?

The leader asks another person in the group to read the passage for the third stage of the process. Before the reading begins, the leader reminds the group members that while they listen to the reading of the passage and during the two to three minutes of silence that follows, they should consider the question, "Do I sense that this passage is inviting me to do or be something in the next few days? Is there encouragement or an invitation to me here, not so much for some long-term project but for something I might do or be in the next day or two? Concretely, what do I sense this passage is calling me to do or be right now?"

The designated person then slowly reads the passage once, and the members of the group ponder this invitation in two to three minutes of silence. Then once more the leader brings the silence to a close by inviting members to share what they sense from the passage. This time the sharing may be somewhat lengthier, as each participant desires. During this sharing, members pay particular attention to what the person to their right says, since they will pray for that person when the group completes its sharing. Once again, anyone who wishes may pass.

The group's responsibility is to receive whatever persons share respectfully and prayerfully, without comment. Probably there will be a keen sense of God's presence; by respectful listening, the group indicates its confidence that God is cherishing each speaker in this very moment—however joyful or painful, sorrowful or confused, loved or lost the speaker feels.

Example

Sharon asks Ann to read this time. Before Ann begins, Sharon briefly instructs the group: "This time we are listening to the passage with the question in our minds, 'Do I sense here an invitation to do or be something in the next few days?'—not meaning by the end of my life but within the coming week. Is there something I am invited or encouraged to do or be?" Ann reads the passage and there is silence.

Sharon brings the silence to a close by asking the group members to share at greater length if they wish, anything each feels invited by the passage to do or be. She also reminds them that they may pass if they prefer.

After another twenty seconds of silence, Charles says hesitantly: "I am struck by the fact that the two disciples call Jesus 'Teacher.' This last month I've been really struggling with whether to stay with high school teaching or to try for a job that pays more and has less personal stress. You all know that I feel this school district is a nightmare of political maneuvering, and it doesn't really value its teachers. What might it mean to be a teacher like Jesus was? I don't feel I'm getting any "answers" from the passage, but I do want to ponder this question seriously over the next week: What does it mean to be a teacher like Jesus, and could I do that?"

Bill responds, "Boy, does that ever make sense to me! My word was "What do you want?" and that really applies to my situation right now. I just don't know what I want, . . . or maybe I want it all! I've got a responsibility to bring in enough income to support my family, and I really get a kick out of the challenges in the banking industry, but these long days and frequent trips take all my energy. I feel like a money-making machine. I never get to enjoy Mary and the kids! Maybe it's unrealistic to want that. All I see to do is keep on doing what I'm doing."

Jim looks like he's about to give Bill some advice, but Sharon motions to him to wait. After a few moments of silence, Mary says, "I'm in such a different place. The guys seem to be so logical and articulate, but for me it is more personal. I was thinking about John the Baptist's sending his disciples to Jesus, and it made me want to cry. You work so hard to get a little acknowledgment of your own value; and then before you've had a chance to appreciate it, you have to give it away! It's John who I want to come and see; I want to talk with him about what it's like to have to give up something precious. I choose to do that—to have an imaginative talk with John the Baptist!"

Ann's eyes are filling with tears. She opens her mouth a couple of times before words will come, then mumbles: "Jesus is so far away, and it's such a struggle to follow him." She says no more, and her tears are under control now. Mary reaches out and squeezes Ann's hand. Sharon murmurs something about "the gift of tears in God's presence."

Jim is looking uncomfortable. He snorts out: "Pass."

Sharon says, "I often find things too difficult or confusing for me to really know what to do—even leading this *lectio*, for example. But I guess the invitation I sense for myself is to stay with Jesus, to keep my hand in his, and to walk forward into the difficulty or confusion as best I can, watching to see what he will do."

Stage Four: Pray

When all have shared or passed, the leader begins the time of prayer. The leader reminds the group that while only one person at a time is formally praying, each one praying is doing so on behalf of the whole group, which jointly holds up the person before God. It helps for each person to say amen at the completion of his or her prayer. The group then echoes that amen to reinforce the awareness that it is the whole group's prayer at every moment.

The purpose of the prayer is simply to affirm God's desire to enable response to the invitation. The one praying also may include a few words of personal thanksgiving for the brother or sister to the right; but at this time, the prayer's focus is simply on acknowledging that the prayers of those present and God's own call support the individual's desire to be more faithful.

The leader begins by praying for the person on her or his right hand, after which the person on the leader's left prays for the leader, and so on sequentially around the circle. Members may choose to pray silently rather than aloud when it's their turn. The person may best serve the group process by announcing that intention and closing with amen so the next person knows when to begin. Allow a moment of silence at the completion of the prayers and then adjourn.

Example

Sharon states "Let's take a time of prayer now, offering up to our God all the things that have surfaced in our hearts and minds in the last few minutes. We are all praying for one another, of course, but one of us will be formally responsible to pray for one other— the person on our right hand—on behalf of the whole group. Our prayer is that each may be empowered to follow through in what he or she has been invited to do or be. I'll begin.

"Our God, I thank you for our brother Bill and his great energy. I thank you that he is asking what he really wants, and I pray that you will help him be discerning as he goes about those tasks he is responsible for in the next week. Amen." All repeat amen.

Mary prays, "Father/Mother God, you have blessed Sharon with your gentleness; give her now strength to face unknown situations in the power of your Spirit. Amen." All repeat amen.

Ann whispers, "Lord, be good to Mary. Amen." All repeat amen.

Charles says, "I'll pray silently." He does so for a few moments, taking Ann's hand in his as he does. He says "Amen," and all repeat it, including Ann.

Jim prays, "Lord Jesus Christ, you provide the model for us of a righteous life; you alone are holy; you are our judge and our savior. Your teachings are full of wisdom, and I pray you'll show

Charles how to be wise too. In your holy name I pray. Amen." All repeat amen.

Bill prays, "Father, I offer my friend Jim to you. You know better than I all the desires of his heart, but I pray that you will help him follow your lead. Amen." All repeat amen.

There is a moment of companionable silence, before persons begin to stretch and to talk softly. Several walk over and hug Ann. Gradually they all head for the kitchen to set out dinner..

Summary

That's the group *lectio* process. The outline on the next page summarizes it for your quick reference. *Lectio* has the simplicity of the gospel and the implicit challenge the gospel carries to make it a vital relaity in every person's life.

Avoid the temptation to elaborate on this basic framework. *Lectio*'s great power resides in its ability to balance elements of activity and receptivity, using silence as a gentle and unhurried way to open each human heart to God's Word. May you be blessed by its practice!

The Group *Lectio* Process

Prepare

Take a moment to come fully into the present. Sit comfortably alert, close eyes, and center yourself with breathing.

1. Hear the word (that is addressed to you).

First reading (twice). Listen for the word or phrase from the passage that attracts you. Repeat it over softly to yourself during a one-minute silence. When the leader gives the signal, say aloud only that word or phrase (without elaboration).

2. Ask, "How is my life touched?"

Second-stage reading. Listen to discover how this passage touches your life today. Consider possibilities or receive a sensory impression during the two minutes of silence. When the leader gives the signal, speak a sentence or two perhaps beginning with the words *I hear, I see, I sense.* (Or you may pass.)

3. Ask, "Is there an invitation here?" (for you).

Third-stage reading. Listen to discover a possible invitation relevant to the next few days. Ponder it during several minutes of silence. When leader gives signal, speak of your sense of invitation. (Or you may pass.)

4. Pray (for one another's empowerment to respond).

Pray, aloud or silently, for God to help the person on your right respond to the invitation received.

If desired, group members may share their feelings about the process after completing these steps.

2 Our heart and Rhythm

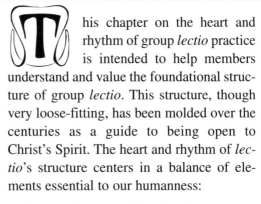

his chapter on the heart and rhythm of group *lectio* practice is intended to help members understand and value the foundational structure of group *lectio*. This structure, though very loose-fitting, has been molded over the centuries as a guide to being open to Christ's Spirit. The heart and rhythm of *lectio*'s structure centers in a balance of elements essential to our humanness:

- the material and spiritual realms;
- activity and receptivity;
- word and silence;
- community life supporting individuals.

Balance is the key to these elements. The heart and rhythm of praying the scriptures involves a continuing, organic interchange or counterpoint among various elements crucial to our wholeness as humans. If we are not particularly attentive to these balances, we may be practicing *lectio* without its heart!

This chapter will explore these four-balanced elements that lie at the center of praying the scripture, its heart and rhythm,

29

to reveal the implicit structure of *lectio*. It will set forth the theoretical basis for *lectio*'s balanced structure, which corresponds to the four elements listed above. Our imaginary group members continue their sessions and demonstrate *lectio* at work.

Attentiveness to the heart and rhythm allows deeper encounter with the living God. However, *lectio*'s structure is somewhat foreign to modern lifestyles. We usually find it necessary to discipline ourselves in order to stay attentive to its heart and rhythm. Certain practical disciplines are essential for fidelity to the heart and rhythm of praying the scriptures. These practical disciplines do not correspond directly to the theoretical balances explored in the rest of the chapter, but they are implicit in all of them. Therefore, it may help to set them out here at the beginning. They are as follows:

- Stay with the words of the passage. (Don't theologize or generalize.)
- Stay with the outline of the process. (Don't elaborate or skip any parts.)
- Take time to prepare and to close every session. (Consent to be here and not somewhere else.)
- Stay open to the unknown. (Watch with awe.)

The heart and rhythm of praying the scriptures require the integration of balance and discipline. Let's explore this further.

The Material and Spiritual Realms

Lectio is founded in a Christian theology that takes the principle of incarnation quite seriously, not only as it applies to God's work and life but also as it expresses a basic truth about human life: God invites us to share in the divine life, even as we go about our everyday activities! The Hebrew Scriptures vividly express incarnation at the moment of human creation—when God breathes spirit into dust:

> Then the Lord God formed man from the dust of the ground, and breathed into his nostrils the breath of life; and the man booame a living being

—Genesis 2:7

Incarnation takes its highest form in the New Testament with the birth of Jesus, fully human and fully divine:

> The Holy Spirit will come upon you [Mary], and the power of the Most High will overshadow you; therefore the child to be born will be holy; he will be called Son of God.

> —Luke 1:35

And God intends that this gift of Christ—the union of divine and human—include rather than exclude us. Through Christ, God invites us to share in the divine life! This is a central message of God's action in creation and in Christ's birth. It is almost too much to take in! It means that our own wholeness requires nurture of the dual aspects of our being: divine and human, spirit and body.

Lectio is designed specifically to help us do this. It engages both our active abilities (expressing our human strengths) and our receptive abilities (expressing our need for the divine spirit or inspiration). Praying the scriptures turns rhythmically to one and then to another in an oscillation similar to that of heartbeat or breath, where material and spiritual are essential elements of a unified process.

Before we can effectively practice balancing the material and spiritual realms in our attempts to pray the scriptures, we first need to acknowledge that our culture does not model the incarnational principle well. At one extreme, our cultural outlook is materialistic: We are fundamentally skeptical of any experience that others cannot measure and verify. We often assume that only the "sensible" exists. As a result, we need both practice and support to trust our *lectio* experiences of God when they transcend the senses.

The "New Age" alternative approach to contemporary living basically goes to the other extreme: It emphasizes spiritual realities by displacing material ones. This outlook presumes that the visible or bodily (that is, the normal struggle of daily life) is illusory and that people only suffer because they allow themselves to get stuck in unreal appearances. As a result, we may feel guilty and somehow "unspiritual" if we are in pain or grief.

Both of these cultural portraits are caricatures, of course, but each is faithful to the implicit and powerful message of our culture: The nuts and bolts of daily life bear no relationship to a spiritual journey; and if we are to gain anything "real" through spiritual growth, it will only be in some distant and amorphous twilight zone. The insistent message is that there is no authentic transforming spiritual power in the midst of material life.

Lectio puts this supposition to the test as it weaves a way through life that insists on balance and integration of the material and the spiritual. Although praying the scriptures involves contemplation, or resting in the wordless experience of God, it also involves mission, or being sent from the embrace of God to the embrace of our actual life experiences to discover how God is present there also. The experience of praying the scriptures involves a back-and-forth flow between the material and the spiritual, which creates new possibilities in the here and now and manifests the inherent union of divine and creaturely elements. Thus *lectio* directly challenges our dominant worldview.

The problem for Christians is that when we take the fullness of our faith seriously, seeking to deny neither the material nor the spiritual dimensions of our actual experience, we are moving into uncharted waters. We are behaving "oddly," somewhat like sailing out across the seas when everyone knows that the earth is flat! To rely on God and follow God's daily guidance is hard work; it requires great discipline and willingness to learn. *Lectio* invites us to do just that and gives us the means to practice it, for its basis is an integration of life experience and the gifts of God.

The following example shows how our tendency to expect life experience to be purely physical or purely spiritual can interfere with effective *lectio*.

Example

The group of six is meeting (a month later) at Jim and Ann's home. On the drive over, Charles says to Sharon, "You know, I really don't get this *lectio* business. We're supposed to start by listening for a word of God, but frankly, I don't know what God sounds like! Isn't this whole process a little like self-hypnosis?"

Sharon nods. "It does seem kind of like a leap in the dark to act as if God really wants to speak to me about my ordinary life issues! But when I just give myself to the process, something happens! Usually 'God's voice' sounds very much like my own, but the insights I get are so practical and so freeing, I'm glad to stay with it."

"Is it important that I pay attention to these reservations of mine?" Charles asks. "Or do you think I should just forget them and plunge in?"

"Maybe both!" Sharon replies. "It seems important that all of us be clear about where we really are on this issue and not try to force something artificial. But for me, there's such a yearning inside; I need something more than already exists in my life. I want more, and I don't know how to get it except by trying out a process I have reason to trust and watching what happens."

Charles grins ruefully. "Yeah, Sharon, who knows but what God can work even through self-hypnosis! I'll hang in there awhile!"

Meanwhile at the house, Mary and Bill have arrived early, and Ann and Mary are talking upstairs. Ann confesses, "This *lectio* is so different from my usual way of prayer that I hardly know what to make of it. You know that for the last year I've been practicing a form of meditation where I have learned to clear my mind of all thoughts. It seems wrong somehow just to let thoughts come in; and when they are about the problems in my life, I feel like I lose my peace completely, and all prayer just leaves me.

Mary sympathizes, "Oh, that must be so troubling!" Her youngest child distracts her for a moment and then she turns back to Ann, "I wonder if maybe prayer has a wider range than we have imagined before? Maybe it includes both that deep inner peace you've found *and also* something that seems more like inner disturbance but is a way of opening the tough issues of our lives directly to God? What do you think?"

Ann says, "Well, maybe. I guess it's worth a try. But it is really hard for me."

In this example, Charles represents the "materialist" view—a thing needs to be tangible in order to be "real," and Ann represents the "spiritualist" view—we are really only in God's presence when we feel calm and remote from practical problems. It helps to acknowledge the assumptions we bring to our practice of praying the scriptures. If we don't know where we are, we can never find our way home. We always begin with the acceptance of what is, along with the unwillingness to allow those understandings to confine us. Group members and individuals start with respect for present dispositions and encourage gentle openness to discover what actually is present and possible.

Internal disquiet caused by seeing the world's viewpoint set beside the biblical one in relation to oneself is often a sign of genuine desire to transcend cultural limits. It is not necessarily negative and need not be stopped or fixed as soon as possible. Inner disquiet may be the way in which we grow beyond our presuppositions or express our hope for possibilities we cannot even imagine. A supportive group that lovingly accepts a wide range of experiences and biases frees members to test their fragile longings for fullness of life. New life comes through the practice of patience and gentleness (even with oneself!), rather than argument or harangue or acting as one thinks one should.

Activity and Receptivity

In *lectio*, we are seeking to be transformed into Christ. That transformation is gradual and grounded in daily life experiences, so it is often invisible to us while it is happening. Only afterward do we look back to observe how much change God has worked in us. We refer to this ongoing and largely invisible work of *lectio* as "formation," meaning the kind of slow but precise shaping of clay by a potter. Yet even the image of a potter is not quite apt, because God does not move to shape us without our own willingness to be shaped. Praying the scriptures involves a balance of activity and receptivity: We actively seek God's hand; we are receptive to gradual shaping. We are conscious and cooperative clay, engaging our will with God's in a process of spiritual formation.

We have difficulty distinguishing between "will" and "willingness." The Hebrew Scriptures avoided our difficulty by speaking of the *heart* as the locus of the active-receptive relationship with God in spiritual formation. For the early Hebrews, the heart involved not just activity but also receptivity. They viewed the heart as the inner seat of the human's whole being. As such, it was the organ of capacity for God's very self: It was the locus not only of choice and motive but also of one's fundamental orientation toward life. In the heart, we are formed and reformed into the person we most long to be. So the psalmist cries out his deep desire for personal transformation in these simple words:

> [O God,] give me understanding, that I may keep your law and observe it with my whole heart.

> —Psalm 119:34

When we consider this place in ourselves that is designed for active receptiveness to God, the place that gradually expresses and develops our unique wholeness, we realize that much of its work is hidden from us. Though central to our being, the heart is out of sight. The physical reality that this essential organ of life is hidden deep within the human body reveals a spiritual truth. Its minute-by-minute rhythmic motion is foundational for our very life, yet ultimately mysterious. Our spiritual heart, like our physical heart, receives aid from our supportive actions (regular exercise, sound diet, and so on), but it is finally beyond our control.

Oddly enough, we express and cooperate with (or resist) this God-receptive, active center of the heart or the will primarily in practical and "unimportant" ways: in the routine decisions of each day, in the motives we use and the desires we pursue, in the development of those habits of speech and action that cumulatively form our temperament and disposition. We develop our capacity for God most directly not so much by our intellect or by our emotions as in our habits and predispositions to action, our choices and our wishes.

Lectio's structure is designed to form this essential center of our being, which is our capacity for God, our disposition to act, our heart/will. *Lectio* asks that we lay our life issues alongside the patterns described in scripture and find there a template that helps us be who we are fully meant to be. *Lectio* takes thought and emotion and intentionally balances them in relationship to our capacity for God. Spiritual growth is fulfilled in the harmony of our will and God's; praying the scriptures enlarges the heart, which is the capacity for such harmony. The model of such growth is Christ, whose will was so attuned to the Father's that both mutually resided in each other.

A life lived from the heart with activity and receptivity in balance is uncommon in our culture. It is risky to undertake the work of the heart with God. Yet *lectio* urges the fruitfulness of this risk, inviting us to live to the fullest.

The following example suggests how praying the scriptures encourages formation through a balance of activity and receptivity. The basic *lectio* structure allows persons to practice the essential mix of action and release safely and in good time. *Lectio*'s reflective structure allows each person to test life experience from the heart gradually; that is, in accordance with God's will.

Example

The group has gathered in Jim and Ann's living room. Mary is tonight's leader. She has begun to review the basic format of *lectio* when Charles interrupts, "Oh, Mary, we know the rules! Let's just move on to the scripture!" Mary looks annoyed but immediately begins to read the passage for tonight Mark 1:35-37:

> In the morning, while it was still very dark, [Jesus] got up and went out to a deserted place, and there he prayed. And Simon and his companions hunted for him. When they found him, they said to him, "Everyone is searching for you.

As soon as Mary finishes reading, Charles says, "Everyone." Bill responds, "In the morning." Ann's word is "prayed." Jim mentions "very dark." Sharon's word is "hunted"; Mary says, "A deserted place."

Then Mary states, "I think we were supposed to have a time of silence listening with our words before we shared anything. This next time, please wait in the silence until I give the signal before you say anything."

She asks Charles to read the passage for the second stage. There is silence after the reading until Mary says, "Okay, now please briefly share if you wish about how this passage seems to touch your life today."

Jim says, "*Dark* was my word, and I'm really in the dark

about this process. I don't see how this nonsense is supposed to get us in touch with God at all."

Ann voices her thought, "Maybe we should take time now to talk with Jim about his concern?" Mary quickly responds, "Let's go ahead with our process as planned and then save time at the end for all of us to talk about how it's going for us generally. Okay?" There are a few nods and then some more silence.

The group continues with the process: Individuals share how they feel touched, hear the reading for the third stage, silently listen until the signal and then share any sense of invitation. Finally each prays for the person on his or her right. They close by praying the Lord's Prayer together.

Mary asks, "Before we get up, let's take a few minutes to talk together about the process of *lectio*. How is it going for us?"

Jim acknowledges, "Well, I find I'm kinda fighting it because it is so unlike my previous experience with the Bible, and I miss thinking about things in a systematic way. But I was really taken by surprise in the middle of our session tonight. At first I was irritated that you didn't stop and talk about what was bothering me. But as we continued to be together with the scripture and the companionable silence, a mantle of peace just seemed to drop down over my shoulders—almost as if God were putting his arm around my shoulder. I still feel in the dark—I didn't get any ideas at all—but suddenly it occurred to me that God may be more than all my ideas about him. The peace I felt was so real! I guess what I really need to do is just stay with this stuff long enough to give it a fair chance."

Charles jumps in. "Yeah, Jim, I was just talking with Sharon about my discomfort before the meeting. This *lectio* stuff is real different but also very moving for me. I still don't know whether I'm making it all up in my own mind or what, but I'd like to keep with it for . . . what—maybe six months—before I decide. By the way, Mary, I realize I was really out of line trying to move you along quickly tonight. Something about repeating those instructions actually helps me simmer down and get present and relaxed, open to whatever will happen here."

Mary replies, "Thanks, Charles. It's not easy to be leader and to know exactly what is important about this procedure. And it is very difficult for me not to jump in when I sense someone is hurting, like I was concerned that Jim might be tonight. I've wondered if the formal structure sometimes prevents us from offering one another the support that we came for. But tonight as I kept us on task with the format, I somehow felt that the *lectio* process itself gave me an important *new* way to give support and to get it."

Sharon adds, "I think we all feel some comfort and some discomfort with *lectio*. But I'm also sensing that we don't really think we will get what it offers until we've tried it for a while."

Ann says, "I'm also having some difficulty with *lectio*; it's not easy for me to let words and images from my life come into my prayer time. I get all jangled, and I feel as if I've lost God. But when I leave here, I feel just as centered as I do in my meditative prayer, and I really appreciate having some people to share the journey with me. So I'm glad we're doing it."

The *lectio* process has an integrity of its own, related to its objective of enlarging the heart for God through balance of action and reception. This means it may raise mild discomfort of various sorts but also that it is amenable to a fair test. Stay with it and be attentive to what is happening. Continually return to the basic directions, and remain as close to them as possible, while also allowing enough flexibility that you don't squeeze God out. We are seeking formation in God's spirit, and *lectio* is intended to increase our receptivity to that Spirit.

Word and Silence

The third element of *lectio*'s heart and rhythm is balance of word and silence. *Lectio*'s structure powerfully balances both. It is rooted in word: It begins with the word of scripture and seeks the Word as Son. It is interacting continuously with the "word" of our personal lives; that is, with our thoughts, dreams, fears, worries, delights.

In the beginning was the Word, and the Word was with God,

and the Word was God. . . . What has come into being in him
was life, and the life was the light of all people.

—John 1:1, 3-4

Lectio is also rooted in silence. We prepare for *lectio* by releasing
outer and inner noise. We begin and end *lectio* with rest in God, receiving without comment whatever is given. In *lectio* sharing, we
speak only the actual words that are born out of our silent pondering
while enfolded in God's life:

> I wait for the Lord, my soul waits, and in his word I hope;
> my soul waits for the Lord more than those who watch for
> the morning, more than those who watch for the morning.

—Psalm 130:5-6

The balance of word and silence is incredibly difficult for us to sustain because our culture is so oriented toward word and so ignorant
of silence. Wherever we go, noise bombards us: elevators, shopping
malls, offices, waiting on the telephone, car radios—everywhere!
Most of us have little or no experience of silence, and we may find
it disturbing or alien. One minute of silence in a public meeting,
even at church, can seem intolerably long. We seem to think that silence is the absence of something, and our nature abhors a vacuum.
Yet we might wonder whether our near-frantic efforts to surround
ourselves with noise suggest a deeper fear—that silence is the presence of something so powerful that it is to be feared.

Yet silence is essential for listening. How awkward to try to
have a serious conversation with someone wearing earphones! How
hard to communicate a message to one wielding a leaf blower! How
impossible to reach someone absorbed in a television program! In
any relationship there must be listening for there to be communication, and that is no less true of our relationship with God than any
other.

With God, we speak our needs, our longings, our hungers, our
pain, our hope. And then we listen, because we speak all these things
in the hope of being *heard* by God. We speak because we need something that we cannot supply ourselves. We speak because we long for
new life, which is beyond our capacity to bring to our experience.

And yet we sense, we pray, that new life is possible for us; that somehow the divine can penetrate the earthly in our particular case, that there is something better and different for us just out of our reach. So in prayer, we also listen. We wait. We quiver in expectancy that God will respond to us.

Word in prayer is our self-giving. Silence in prayer is receptivity to the self-giving of God. The balance of the two creates possibilities in our midst beyond our imagining! *Lectio* is rooted in this formative balance of word and silence.

Example

Our group of six has met now over several months, and they are beginning to be more relaxed with the process. Tonight they are at Bill and Mary's home, and Jim is leading. They have just heard the first double reading of the passage:

> Treasure up my commandments within you, making your ear attentive to wisdom and inclining your heart to understanding; . . . cry out for insight.

> —Proverbs 2:1-2, 3

There is a minute of silence, and then Jim invites people to share the word that came to them. Charles says, "Salvation."

After a moment of silence, Jim asks, "Is there a direct word from the passage itself that you also heard, Charles?" Charles looks up, surprised, and after a moment says, "Uh, treasure."

Sharon says, "Incline." Ann mentions the phrase "inclining your heart." Bill responds, "Understanding." Mary utters, "Cry out"; Jim says, "Commandments."

Jim asks group members to listen in the silence for the way the passage touches their lives. Mary reads the passage a second time. After about twenty seconds, Ann blurts out, "I'm trying to figure out how the heart can be inclined. Does that mean it is turned on its side or turned around or at an angle or what? And if the heart is not in the right inclination, does it mess up the other

internal organs? I mean, would there be a lung problem or something like that? Sometimes I really have trouble breathing. . . . "

Jim touches Ann's hand and says, "Let's just take a bit more
time in the silence, and see what it tells us." Ann blushes, and sub-
sides into silence. When Jim invites sharing about a minute later,
Charles says, "I thought of going to heaven and finding a big pile of
gold there just for me. Is salvation like a big pile of gold? Surely not!
But what does salvation mean? What is treasure? It's confusing."

Ann passes, and Bill shares, "Well, I got the picture of a
mathematical equation representing understanding. I realize that
doesn't offhand seem to make much sense, but I think it probably
comes from my extensive analytical training. Equations stand for
the means by which we come to understanding."

Jim says, "Thanks, Bill."

All three of these responses are ways of overbalancing *lectio* in favor
of word. Charles chose a concept (salvation) to interpret the scripture instead of a word from the scripture itself. Ann jumped in before the leader gave the signal, anxious to pour out whatever was
beginning to emerge before it had time to grow into fullness in the
silence. And Bill felt compelled to explain or rationalize why he had
received the image that came.

All of these responses have a place, but *lectio* is not that place.
There are times for activity and responsibility, but *lectio* is designed to
help us gain access to those new resources beyond ourselves, which are
available only in receptivity. In *lectio* we are seeking that transformation
into Christ, which comes as gift to those who wait in need and longing.
In *lectio*, we let a new and powerful word be born in the soil of silence
by following the common procedures that facilitate this balance.

And, of course, there can be imbalance toward silence as well
as imbalance toward word.

Example

The group continues the sharing after the second-stage reading.
This time Jim says, "I'm in such a peaceful, imageless place that
I'm finding words intrusive. I pass."

Sharon expresses, "I sometimes think I would prefer to be in a convent where I could spend all day turning my ear to wisdom."

And Mary concludes, "When I think of the circumstances of my life, I want to cry out in anger and pain. I would rather not think of them but just be here in this warm fellowship for a while, forgetting all that other stuff."

These responses tend toward imbalance in the other direction. The desire to escape is understandable and is often healing in small doses, but the goal of *lectio* is the integration of life and prayer. *Lectio* intends that we bring to bear in word/activity those inner certainties experienced in silence/rest. In *lectio*, we seek to experience rest in order to let it inform our daily struggles, decisions, and actions. When we refuse to let the gospel illumine our present life situation honestly and lovingly, we are retreating from this essential pole of life's activity and thus losing a necessary human balance. Our lives are to be changed by our faith; for this to happen, we must inquire of our actual life experiences how faith gently informs and empowers them.

The element of silence in *lectio* brings opportunity to let our few words be genuinely formed from the receptive encounter with God. The element of word acknowledges that our encounter with God empowers and sends us to be God's life in the world, while helping us be specific about what that might mean to us today.

Community Life Supporting Individuals

The form of *lectio* we are using is set within a small Christian community where we can mutually support one another while we navigate the testing waters of the presence of Christ's living Spirit in our midst. We usually find that when we commit ourselves to spiritual growth, we long for practical support and accountability to others who share our commitment to Christ. We have a deep desire to be known by others as we really are; that is, as we are known by Christ, celebrating our real strengths and complementing our real weaknesses. We long to talk with others about things that really confuse us, as well as about things that really delight us. Few places in our world offer this opportunity, but an authentic small group is one of them. Thus a Christian small group is an ideal setting, a means of true community life, for the practice of *lectio*.

Although small groups seem to be sprouting up all over, they are often disappointing or of short duration. A central problem is that our culture tends to be hostile not only to things spiritual but also to things communal. We live and breathe in a setting that exalts individualism and rewards independence. Indeed, we commonly react to words like *community*, *commitment*, and *dependence* with wariness, anticipating limits on our freedom. We do not really know how to trust one another, how to support one another in pain, how to disagree in love, how to genuinely respect one another, how to be "for" one another in the long haul. While a *lectio* group only requires a short-term and limited range of commitment, it does call us to practice skills that are generally undeveloped among us—skills that balance community and individual needs.

Lectio creates a bond among group members that truly manifests the body of Christ. Saint Paul describes the nature of this body: It has many different parts, each important as itself, that somehow contribute to the whole. In Christ, we come to know one another as kin, united in our love and longing for God, however great our diversity. After a few months, we might find ourselves surprised that while we may not yet have discovered "basic" things about others in the group (such as how many children they have or what their jobs are), we feel like brothers and sisters in a shared love that has existed forever.

Today we know a great deal about fellowship and about psychological needs, but we have remarkably little experience of Christian community; that is, of being the body of Christ. In Christ, we care for one another *in the context* of awareness that God is doing more for each of us than any of us can desire or even imagine! This awareness of God's care does not exempt us from the responsibility of being a caring community, but it does relieve us of the compulsive serving that so often distracts us from our own responsibility to and direct engagement with God. In our gathered community, a Spirit is at work that is more powerful than any individual care and that is deeply engaged with every single one of us. The community of

Christ's body is one in which we know one another through the eyes of Christ, as it were. This relationship differs from our usual way of experiencing one another. There is something radically distinctive about such mutual knowing.

Group *lectio* allows us to practice together what it is to grow into this balanced community, this body of Christ. The key to balance in Christian community life is this: Whatever is happening in any person at this moment, Christ is now active in its bringing forth life and giving growth. In order to practice this balance regularly, we need specific tools to keep ourselves on course. Four practices help us make Christ the center of our *lectio* community life so that our group is actively supporting individuals in their unique spiritual journeys:

- speaking the truth in love,
- admitting strong emotions,
- listening in love,
- confidentiality.

These four practices, explored in the following sections, are a necessary part of the covenanting and leadership tools discussed in chapter 3.

Speaking the Truth in Love

Speaking the truth in love, we must grow up in every way into him who is the head, into Christ, from whom the whole body [is] joined. . . . So then, putting away falsehood, let all of us speak the truth to our neighbors, for we are members of one another.

—Ephesians 4:15-16, 25

In a healthy body, each part must be itself as fully as possible, while aiding the other parts to become what they are. Among other things, this means learning to live and speak—as much as possible—the truth in love. For example, if one ankle is badly sprained but pretends it is not; nevertheless, you will place additional strain on the other leg and possibly areas of the back to compensate. Or we might be strongly right-handed, but implicit overreliance upon that strength causes gradual deterioration in left-hand capability. If we could imagine parts of the body acting to deceive one another, such that all the affected parts are making difficult adjustments but pretending they are not, we can get some idea of how dishonesty pervades and distorts community life.

Thus, a balanced community life depends in part on our mutual commitment to work toward truthfulness in our relationships with one another and God. Truthfulness does not mean making ourselves unnecessarily vulnerable, nor does it mean verbally assaulting others. But it does mean speaking without deliberate deception; sharing our own thoughts, feelings, and dreams as fully as we feel able; and mirroring as accurately as possible what we hear from others. Truthfulness means speaking for ourselves and taking responsibility for our own ideas and feelings, as well as being aware of and remaining connected in love through disagreements.

Unity in diversity is a goal not easily realized, and it helps to recognize that we are working toward it (in the power of the Spirit), rather than inheriting it ready made in our Christian groups.

Lectio groups are a means to seek the Word of God in order to bring it into our lives. God's Word is obviously vibrant, multifaceted, powerful, and often challenging. The goal of *lectio* is to incarnate this transforming Word in such a way that increasingly we are able to give it forth as our own personal truth. This discipline is strenuous, but we may practice speaking the truth in love in several basic ways in our *lectio* groups: First, always speak with "I" messages; express your own feelings, doubts, and desires rather than talking about what others need or giving advice. Second, welcome conflict as a means of gaining a better perspective on the whole.

Example

Our group of six has gathered at the home of Sharon and Charles for a *lectio* meeting and has listened for the second time to this reading:

> Above all, clothe yourselves with love, which binds everything together in perfect harmony. And let the peace of Christ rule in your hearts, to which indeed you were called

in the one body. And be thankful. Let the word of Christ
dwell in you richly.

—Colossians 3:14-16

Tonight Bill is leading, and when he gives the go-ahead to share
something of how members' lives have been touched, Jim begins,
"My word is *perfect harmony*, and I can't help but reflect on how
little harmony there is in the church. They bicker all the time
about unimportant things and never set aside time for important
things like Bible study. That's why I joined this group, and I think
every member of the church should join one too!"

Bill asks simply, "Is there something in particular that
touches *you* about perfect harmony, Jim?"

Jim exclaims, "Yes, of course, that's what I'm saying: I really miss it!"

Mary responds, "My word was *be thankful*. And my experience of our church is different from Jim's, because in the silence
I felt myself a part of a circle dance—so many friends from
church holding hands and dancing together with Jesus at the center of the circle. And I am filled with gratitude."

The time of *lectio* itself is not a time for extended conversation, neither about the personal nature of Jim's reactions nor about a difference of viewpoint between Jim and Mary. But it is important to be
moving toward a deepened ability to speak the truth in love in all of
our exchanges; that is a primary means by which we become members of Christ's body to one another. In our *lectio* groups, we have
an opportunity to practice what communication might be like when
genuinely formed by the Word of God. This does not mean constant
agreement or even lukewarm tolerance but rather a commitment to
valuing ourselves and others, aware that in some way we are given
to one another to be who we really are. In *lectio*, we practice the root
meaning of *benediction*: *bene* means "good" or "well," and *dicere*
means "to speak." So when we speak well, when we speak the truth
in love, we are a source of blessing to one another. We intend the best
for one another, as well as for ourselves.

Admitting Strong Emotions

Reflecting on speaking the truth in love, we realize that it is impossible to speak the truth if we are not living the truth. We can only communicate that which we have allowed to become conscious in ourselves; we can only speak what we know because we are living it. It is not easy to let the truth about ourselves rise fully into our awareness; for when we do, we often face troublesome facts that we cannot change. For instance, we may be painfully lonely or agonizingly helpless. We are unaccustomed to admitting feelings that we cannot immediately direct toward a solution. And admission means both willingness to allow something to enter our consciousness and willingness to speak or share. The risk of admission is as old as humankind. Many of the psalms speak eloquently of this dilemma:

> In the day of my trouble I seek the Lord; in the night my hand is stretched out without wearying; my soul refuses to be comforted. I think of God, and I moan; I meditate, and my spirit faints.

> —Psalm 77:2-3

As we open the depths of ourselves honestly before God in group *lectio*, we may find strong emotions surfacing in us, and we are encouraged at least to admit them to ourselves, as well as to admit them in the safe context of the group when we are ready. Two frequently experienced emotions are sadness and anger.

In the midst of a *lectio* session, we may find ourselves in tears, pain, awareness of loss and loneliness. We may have an acute sense of incompleteness and inadequacy, or we may admit all that we long for and have not found. It is not surprising that when we experience directly both our need and God's generosity, we receive what the Christian tradition calls "the gift of tears." Yet often these tears are felt to be embarrassing or awkward not only for the one affected but also for the group. Group members may respond by ignoring or covering over the intense emotion: "It will be all right!" Or perhaps we make an attempted rescue, thinking that, having been offered another's pain, we need to fix it.

Yet being together in Christ usually calls for another response. First we simply hear and acknowledge that at least one of us is experiencing pain or grief or limitation. And together on behalf of one who suffers, we offer the woundedness to Christ in our midst, knowing that he is already moving toward healing more fully than we can know. This does not mean that we discard helpful resources we might offer to one another at a later time. It simply means that above all in our *lectio* group we are attuned primarily to Christ's powerful presence active with us now as we come together in his name, and we first turn to him for help.   After acknowledging what is actually occurring, we offer it to Christ among us. We may intensify our silent prayer, attentive to God in our midst and earnestly holding up the one in pain to God's all-gracious embrace. We do not know how God may be working in this suffering. The experience of loss or inadequacy may be a necessary prelude to some important conversion of heart; the sense of incompleteness or restlessness may be a necessary prerequisite to a deeper embrace of God.

Every experience, positive or negative, is just the right thing for us at this moment if we offer it and ourselves to God's mercy. Group *lectio* offers a supportive environment in which to believe *and practice* this great mystery of faith. *Lectio* is a powerful means of mutual support, as we put into practice the understanding that our relationship to one another is *through Christ.*

Example

It is now Ann's turn to share after the second-stage reading of Colossians 3:14-16. She begins to speak, but then she sobs and swallows several times. Finally she gasps for breath and speaks, "That phrase, *the peace of Christ*, is like a dagger in my heart. I have so little peace; I do everything wrong; it's so unfair!" Tears stream down her face, and she says no more. Mary slips over the sofa to give Ann a tissue and put an arm around her.

There is an uncomfortable silence as Ann continues to cry. Bill, the leader, looks awkward and seems unsure of what to do.

Gradually Ann's sobs diminish, and she quiets in Mary's embrace. Although the silence is difficult, no one hurries to end it.

Finally Sharon speaks, "My phrase was *Christ dwell*. In some strange way in these last few moments, I have had an acute sense of Christ's presence right here with us, sharing Ann's pain and uniting us all. It was like Mary's dance but this time a dance of sorrow rather than joy; a gift of being together no matter what." Ann's eyes meet Sharon's, and a look of understanding passes between them.

A second strong emotion that may surface in *lectio* is anger. We may feel that God has abandoned us or that we have been placed in a most unfair situation. We may even experience anger directed at one another or the group process because we feel we are not finding what we seek and need from the process. But again, the community in Christ centers its response in respect and a certain detachment. Whatever is happening at the moment is in Christ's hands. The anger may simply need to surface so that it can be dealt with in the relationship with God.

The Psalms often express the conviction that God receives our anger willingly; what is crucial is that we persist in the relationship with God no matter what. The *lectio* group does not need to accept responsibility for the anger nor to resolve it; it needs only to entrust the person and the situation to God, who is present at this moment in the group's midst.

Example

Charles now shares. He shifts uncomfortably and says, "The word I got was *binds*. And right now, I'm feeling pretty tied up. What kind of Christians are we anyway, to sit here helplessly while Ann is feeling such pain? Surely there is something wrong with a process that brings so much junk to the surface! I don't want to be a part of anything that makes people hurt so much!" There is a long, awkward silence.

Jim blurts out, "Aren't we going to respond to Charles?!" Bill shakes his head in confusion and says thoughtfully, "I'm not sure quite what to do now, but if I understand our commitment to one another, the main thing is that we have promised to complete this full *lectio* format each time without jumping to anything else during the time itself. And the reason we do that is because we're convinced that somehow Jesus Christ is here with us in a privileged way, especially revealed in the structure of *lectio*. So if Ann feels okay about it, I propose that we continue and then talk more after we finish if we need to."

Ann nods, and Bill continues. "My word was also *peace of Christ*, and a funny image seemed to come to me during the quiet time. What I got was a sense of about ten kids, all bundled up and playing out in the snow. They were laughing and throwing snowballs and crying and shoving and touching and making lots of noise. And yet—maybe it was the softness of the snow, I don't know—but overall there was the strongest sense of peacefulness and rightness and gladness. It was really a kind of celebration, even though it was nothing like I would normally consider as peace!

"Let's go on now to hear the scripture again, pondering if there is an invitation there for each one of us right now."

Admitting strong emotions is not an easy discipline, and the group may experience some discomfort in doing so. But the admission and offering to Christ here and now express a powerful mode of healing that is generally inaccessible to us if we follow our usual pattern of turning to our own resources at once rather than waiting in trust for the Spirit.

Listening in Love

And [Jesus] said, "Let anyone with ears to hear listen!"

—Mark 4:9

Community life in Christ is based on good listening. One of our most fundamental needs as human beings is to be listened to and understood. Curiously enough, we do not often have this experience. We are more prone to analyze, defend, or attempt to solve the problem rather than simply hearing and acknowledging one another. Carl Rogers has said, "Real communication occurs . . . when we listen with understanding. What does this mean? It means to see the expressed idea and attitude from the other person's point of view, to sense how it feels to him [or her], to achieve his [or her] frame of reference. . . . If I can listen to what another tells me . . . then I will be releasing potent forces of change in him [or her]."[2]

Authentic listening is a creative process. None of us really knows ourselves in God until we have been able to speak and be heard at the level of our spirit. Others mirror back to us what we seldom fully understand alone—the particular reality of each human life hidden with Christ in God. In true listening, we enable one another to discover and affirm this truth about ourselves. We listen to one another's visions and affirm that we are made to become what we behold.

However, it is difficult to begin speaking of these truths. We try to share an aspect of ourselves that seems incredibly personal and precious, and we are inevitably tentative as we touch the sensitive edges of these realities. At this level we notice the slightest nuances of response: any boredom or judgment or disapproval may close us up again for a long time. To give another the gift of listening is to offer a space of real safety and support in which each of us can become the one he or she is meant to be. And so in group *lectio*, we begin listening to one another as persons, long before we can even form the words to express that which is being heard.

We need Christ's help in order to be this kind of listener. All of us invariably bring biases and prejudices and other limitations that keep us from being good listeners. Consequently, an important start to the skill of good listening is self-knowledge, so that we can be extra careful in those areas where we know we find it difficult to hear. And we need always to be praying that God will enable us to be more open. So listening begins with self-understanding and prayer. And we can supplement these basics with a practical approach.

The main "secret" of good listening is to hear what has actually been said and to communicate that we have heard it. In listening, we are not trying to form or express our own opinion, to persuade another, to disprove or defend anything. Rather, we are attentive to what the other is communicating by word and gesture and personal meaning.

For example, if a married couple is talking together, and one says to the other, "I wish you would . . . ," it is a rare spouse who will actually *listen* to the end of the sentence! To listen is to be able to describe in one's own words what it is that the other person is actually saying. Instead, the listener has usually jumped far ahead, either to solve the other's "problem" or to defend against a perceived accusation. We often seem to believe that if we let the other person know that we *understand* what he or she has said, we have somehow bound ourselves to *agreeing*. But in fact, what each of us really desires in conversation is simply *to be heard*. Receiving what we wish may be far less important to us than knowing we have been fully heard.

The main way we express good listening skills in *lectio* is by our prayer at the end, since in general we do not give verbal feedback to one another during the sharing itself. It is also possible to offer one another a brief word of affirmation along with a touch after the session, emphasizing what we *heard*, rather than any advice we might have. (The section on "covenanting" in chapter 3 supplements this discussion on the gift of authentic listening.)

Example

In the same group *lectio* session on Colossians, it is now time for the third period of sharing. Bill asks the group members to share now any invitation they have received and afterward for each to pray for the person on the right.

Mary begins, "I feel an invitation to be sure that each day includes a few moments of celebrating the good things of that day, sort of to make thankfulness more a regular part of my conscious thought."

Ann says quietly, "There is much in my life that is not peaceful but also much that is. Tonight I have experienced the love and support of each of you so strongly, and that means so much. I feel my invitation is to know that, whatever else is going on, I also have *this* place of refuge and care. I'm so grateful to all of you."

Charles says, "I think the invitation to me is not to run away when feelings get strong but to accept that Christ can be present in the pain and anger as much as—maybe even more than—in joy and peace."

Sharon expresses her understanding, "For me the invitation is to be as tender toward my own pain and sorrow as I can be toward the pain of someone I love."

Jim states, "I feel urged to do something to bring better Bible study to the church."

Bill concludes, "I feel invited to explore more how peace can be found in playfulness." Bill pauses briefly. "Now let's pray for each other, silently if we wish but being sure to say 'Amen' when we are finished. . . . God, I pray for Jim, that you will help him share his giftedness in Bible study with others and to discover there the unity in you for which he longs. Amen."

Mary prays, "Father/Mother God, you have given Bill a wonderful vision of play as an expression of your very life. Help him find time and energy to play both as a means of joy and as a way of union with you. Amen."

Ann prays, "Father, I'm so glad you give Mary her wonderful capacity to be thankful; help it grow in her. Amen."

Charles prays, "Jesus, I'm grateful that you have shown me Ann's courage tonight, her courage to face pain without running away. I'm glad too that you have helped her receive the love we all have for her and pray that you will continue to do that every day this week. Amen."

Sharon prays, "Holy Spirit, your ways are often different than ours. Thank you for giving Charles the awareness that you don't leave us but are willing to wrestle with us through all thoughts and feelings. Amen."

Jim prays, "Christ our Lord, you shared our sorrow in your passion and death that we might share your resurrection. I pray especially that you will help Sharon be gentle and accepting of her sorrowing, knowing that you share it with her. Amen."

After a moment, Bill asks, "Do we feel that we want to talk now for a while about tonight's experience?"

Jim replies, "I think Charles and Ann should have a chance to say something." Charles says, "In the last silence, I realized that it wasn't so much what was happening with Ann that upset me as that her evident pain made me aware of my own. And I wanted to run away. But, as I suggested in my prayer, when I stayed here in the silence, I began to be aware not only of Ann's pain but of her courage. I realized that if she didn't need to run away or to cover it over, neither did I. She really taught me something very important, and I think I understand *lectio* better too."

Ann says, "That's kind of you, Charles, although I don't know that I'm aware of having much courage. But I learned something tonight too. Mary's touch and the kind of acceptance all of you expressed for my tears helped me feel that what was happening with me was somehow okay and certainly in God's hands. Oddly enough, the fact that we continued with our *lectio* told me that you had confidence that God *is* here embracing me, and I knew I could believe that too."

Bill says, "It seems that it would be good to sum up all our prayers and our discussion with the Lord's Prayer before we adjourn." And they do so.

There is a kind of humility in being a good active listener. We consent to say what seems obvious in order to let others know that we really care about what they are saying. When we state in our own words what another has communicated, usually it is received as a powerful affirmation. It may seem that this "repetition" contributes nothing, but in practice it helps the speaker to feel both known and accepted. Good listening immeasurably helps to build dynamic and trusting group relationships and to strengthen individual growth in Christ.

And, of course, careful listening to one another is a way of being attentive to God. In group *lectio*, we have gathered to hear the Word of God. We hear this word in the scripture, and we listen attentively to help one another hear it in our own lives. Another sensitive listener is the best aid to help us hear the Spirit at work in us, as participants in spiritual direction have known for centuries. In many ways, a good group *lectio* experience is in fact an experience of group spiritual direction. Let those who have ears to hear listen!

Confidentiality

Lectio is an intimate process. Even when we limit our verbal sharing to a few brief words in the *lectio* process, we find that we are revealing precious and vulnerable parts of ourselves. Our listening to the combination of scripture and Spirit touches chords of our deepest desires as human beings.

Intimacy at this level is risky, involving not only our longing for transformation but also our inevitable recognition of the most broken and least acceptable parts of ourselves. We may fear that others will not treat these sacred parts of ourselves tenderly, or we may not have language to express new awarenesses. For us today, it is certainly easier to talk about money, and perhaps even about sex, than to talk about a vital relationship with God. When we share our spiritual life with others, we become known in a profoundly intimate way; and this depth of community life requires both courage and mutual respect in order to sustain it. Each session's leader and all the other group members share responsibility for maintaining these safe boundaries of courage and mutual respect. Chapter 3 gives more insight into this aspect of the leader's role.

Intimacy cannot and should not be demanded, and it is well for participants to be somewhat cautious at first, taking time to let authentic trust build in the group. Nothing requires that we "bare all" in the first meeting, and prudence suggests that everyone honor a gradual and organic pace in the development of deep mutuality.

Never force sharing. Everyone has permission to pass at any point for any reason or no reason. Often persons pass either because they have heard nothing yet (or what they have heard is not yet formed into words) or because what they have heard is so intimate, so powerful, and perhaps so painful that they are not yet able to speak it. Whatever the reason, the decision to remain silent is best met with respect and with gentleness. Each person knows for him- or herself when sharing is premature and when it is safe. It is vital to group life and individual growth to honor this reticence. Jesus said,

> In everything do to others as you would have them do to you.

> —Matthew 7:12

Above all, confidentiality is essential. Whatever members share in the group should never be spoken of outside the group, unless by the person who shared it. A spouse not present should not be told; members not present this week should not be told what a third party shared, although of course any members may speak of what they themselves said. In general, it is better that group members not speak among themselves about others' sharing or their situations as revealed in previous meetings. We never know how our "innocent" sharing may connect with what others know to create a misleading impression or negative effect.

Yet confidentiality is easier asked for than achieved. We have little practice with it, almost seeming to feel that we have an obligation to tell whatever we know! We may tell ourselves that we speak about another's situation out of concern. While that is often true, we can inadvertently do serious harm by speaking out, even about something that seems to us to be minor. Confidentiality is a genuine prerequisite for the vulnerable sharing involved in *lectio* and thus is an essential part of the group's commitment to one another. Confidentiality enables us to risk faith-sharing with one another, to risk speaking with one another about how we sense God's movement in our lives

The practices of prudence, respect for reticence, and confidentiality do not eliminate the need for courage in sharing. Risk will continue to be a factor in expressing these inner dynamics of faith to others. As we begin to notice and articulate the inner yearnings that express our deepest essence, we are as vulnerable as a newborn child. And we need as much emotional tenderness and care from those with whom we share as does a baby. But in a safe setting, such sharing can truly be life-giving, for together we are best able to affirm and embrace the unique self that is truly our own in Christ.

Example

Our group of six is meeting again, this time at Jim and Ann's home with Jim leading the session. The scripture is Isaiah 42:3:

A bruised reed he will not break, and a dimly burning wick
he will not quench; he will faithfully bring forth justice.

The group has heard the third-stage reading and is sharing whatever invitation the passage seems to hold for them today.

Bill states, "I feel invited to express my thanks for this group. In the past, I have been in groups where something I said in confidence came back to me later in a public forum. I'm really grateful that this has been a place where I can explore my ambivalence about my job without fearing that I'll hear about it from my boss in a few weeks. I'm not sure that I really would want to leave my job, but I have needed a space in which to talk about it openly and let off some steam. I feel like I've been a bruised reed; not only have you been careful not to break me, you are gradually helping the bruises to heal! You've really been there for me, and I'm very thankful."

Sharon says, "I too have often felt like a bruised reed. I'm dealing with so many things in my therapy right now. I really haven't needed to surface all the details here, but I've needed a safe place to practice being who I am. I'm appreciative that no one has forced me to share when I needed to pass, and no one has insisted that I tell more at any moment than I'm able to. I've felt quite free to share all that I wanted to precisely because no one has ever demanded that I share too much! Right now, I think the invitation to me is to recognize the safe places in my life and to risk revealing even more of myself there. I know you have helped me be willing to consider that." Sharing continues and closes in prayer.

As we have explored these practical aspects of community life as the body of Christ, *lectio* begins to come alive. We practice being Christ's body through speaking the truth in love, admitting strong emotions, listening in love, and practicing confidentiality. These practices open us to the discovery of a radical way of being together—unlike that which is generally available in our culture. It brings us into a relationship that is promised in scripture and matched by the longings of our hearts.

As Christians, we are promised a oneness in Christ that also empowers the uniqueness of each person. As we come together in love and truth within the body of Christ that we are, our spiritual growth unfolds naturally as individuals and as community. As we allow ourselves to be known by others as we really are, we also discover more about ourselves as we are known by Christ. As we mutually receive the fullness of individual expression, we come to know what it is to belong to a loving and supportive community. This balance, the experience of community that also supports and strengthens individuals, is a crucial one for effective *lectio*.

Summary

This chapter has revealed the implicit structure of group *lectio*, which is often in contrast with the general cultural environment in which we live. The positive elements built into the structure of *lectio* keep us centered in the process of spiritual growth we embrace. These positive elements are all facets of balance, means of integrating important aspects of our human wholeness. They include integration of the material and spiritual realms, of activity and receptivity, of word and silence, and of community life supporting individuals.

Lectio provides a gentle oscillation between review of the situations of our actual daily life and an offering of them to God, which is a way of setting side by side the material and spiritual dimensions of ourselves in order to facilitate their integration. We are seeking transformation into Christ through the training of our heart for responsiveness to God in the midst of our lives—a blend of action and receptiveness. We sense a need for self-giving as well as openness to receive the self-giving of God. This rhythm is best facilitated by a mix of word and silence. And we find that, although it is hard work, we are much enriched by practicing all this in a small Christian community. The structure of group *lectio* offers a firm yet flexible process that gives genuine mutual support for practical and personal spiritual growth.

In *lectio*, we are living into the possibilities of transformation in our lives. We are being formed into Christ, together as Christ's body, in order to become open to the new life always waiting to emerge where death seems to have triumphed. What a challenge! What an adventure! What an opportunity!

3   Together in Christ

his chapter sets out practical matters integral to a sound group *lectio* process. It supplies basic supplementary information on getting started, optimum group size, foundational mutual covenants, leadership, and so on that help a group to begin and faithfully sustain its practice of *lectio*. The goal of these details is to create a flexible *lectio* structure for a satisfying, growth-inducing and Christ-centered small group process, while also supporting each member in being a Christian in the midst of life. The tools presented here build on and provide a framework for the four elements of community life that support individuals discussed in chapter 2.

Many groups depend upon the presence of a leader figure for their structure and discipline. The leader implicitly sets and maintains the ground rules. However, in an independent and cooperatively led group such as the one recommended here for effective *lectio*, it is necessary for all the group members to share responsibility for the establishment and continuance of group life. In assuming mutual leadership, we may feel a bit out of our depth, a little like Jeremiah:

"Ah, Lord God, truly I do not know how to speak, for I am only [a participant]" (1:6-7).

However, a few basic practices presented here can make this shared group leadership much easier, enabling all *lectio* group members to participate in knowledge and responsibility for group life.

Getting Started

For many of us, the process of getting a group together seems overwhelming, if not impossible. We're not sure how to go about it; we're shy to ask others; we're sure no one will be interested; we feel it may be an imposition; we know it's been tried before . . . the list of anxieties goes on forever. The best way to begin any group is to pray about it. If you have been reading this book and are interested in trying to get a *lectio* group together, consider that God has planted that interest in your heart; and God is probably matching it with some unspoken desire in the hearts of others you know.

The first step of any good action is always praying to God to bring it to perfection. Pray to be open and responsive to what God is calling you to do as the group begins to come into being, and pray specifically that God will bring others to join you. Then everything that follows takes place in the light and under the strength of that prayer—so keep your eyes open!

It is a good idea to find someone to help you in the initial stages. If the vision is yours alone at present, find at least one other who shares your dream and desire for a *lectio* group and work together on it. Decide how many you need at minimum. Five or six is a good starting number; twelve is probably too many for one group.

Think and pray about people you know who might be interested in this kind of experience and propose it to them. Don't presume that people won't be interested: Go ahead and ask them! Talk about your plans with enthusiasm, and invite others to join you. As people agree to join you, ask them to share their enthusiasm with others. Personal contact—sharing the contagion of your excitement—is the best recruiting device. Some people will not be interested for a variety of reasons but don't let that get you down. A few will be delighted, and that's all you need.

When you talk with others, don't understate your hopes or your commitment. Let them know how important you expect the *lectio* group to be for your spiritual journey, and be honest about the level of commitment you will want from members. You may be surprised how many people would rather join a group that really intends a serious (though not solemn) commitment than one that only expects a half-hearted response. Don't underestimate the value of diverse gifts and temperaments in a *lectio* group; sometimes it is much richer with a variety of viewpoints. You'll find that the basic "criterion" you'll want to present to potential members is "Are you really seeking God?"; and then, "Does this particular method seem sufficiently fruitful to you that you would be willing to commit to it for a time?"

When you've gathered enough interested people, decide on a time and place for the first meeting and make sure that everyone can come. The first meeting will be an exploratory one, one in which those present actually practice a *lectio* experience and then discuss possible covenant items (reviewed in the following section). By the end of that meeting, you will want to reach agreement on basic format, timing, and covenant items.

The basic format for regular meetings is flexible, depending on members' needs and desires. A group may wish to combine the *lectio* experience with other elements, such as additional (contemplative or intercessory) prayer time, spiritual reading and study, life sharing and support, joining together in a meal, and/or working together on a service project or common task. It is not impossible to undertake a group *lectio* time before the normal meeting of a regular church committee the parish council, vestry, or board of elders), or to include it as part of a support group agenda. Just be sure to keep the *lectio* process intact, not mixing it with other elements during the period of *lectio* itself.

Consideration of timing involves several elements, including the length of initial commitment as well as the frequency and duration of meetings. The optimum frequency probably is weekly, although the group may decide on something else more suitable for them. The *lectio* process itself will take twenty-five to forty minutes, depending on the size of the group. Of course, the meetings will be correspondingly longer if additional activities are planned. Generally it is good to make an initial commitment to the process for a specific period of months to give it a chance to take hold before attempting to evaluate it.

Before you leave the exploratory meeting, you will want to give everyone present the opportunity to express commitment to the group. And you will want to schedule the next (regular) meeting with those who will join. You're on your way!

Covenanting together

A mutually led group needs to begin with free and frank discussion of people's hopes and what their commitment to one another will be. If several members have different sets of expectations, the result is bound to be less than satisfactory. When we choose to come together in a small group, the promise or covenant we make to one another helps shape and direct our life together. It is as if we were all building a home—a task that is nearly impossible if each person has a different set of plans. "Come to him, a living stone, . . . and like living stones let yourselves be built into a spiritual house" (1 Pet. 2:4, 5). Our covenant helps move us from vague intention to directed and mutual commitment.

Since everyone in the group is to be a full participant with each assuming responsibility for good content and mutual sharing, it is important that all participate fully in negotiating the covenant agreement during the first meeting. The covenant agreement includes basic *lectio* principles and practices as well as practical ground rules established by the group, involving both context and practice of meetings.

The Content of Meetings

Begin the exploratory meeting with a practice of group *lectio*. Then discuss meeting content issues raised in chapter 2, assuring that they are understood and can be accepted by each member or will be modified in some way. Particular issues to be aired and agreed upon include these:

- We will accept ourselves and our lives as we are, but we consent not to be confined by the present.
- We will allow our hearts to be formed by *lectio*'s structure:
  —by staying with the words of the scripture passage,
  —by staying with the outline of the process (in the chart at the end of chapter 1),

—by taking time to prepare and close every session, and
—by staying open to the unknown.
- We will practice a balance of silence and word. We will assure that everyone listens and everyone may speak.
- We will speak the truth in love:
—by speaking for oneself rather than "at" others and
—by welcoming and airing diverse points of view.
- We will admit strong emotions to ourselves and, when appropriate, to others.
- We will practice confidentiality.

The Practice of Meetings

In addition to the content, the covenant will include other practical items. It will be helpful to discuss and agree on an approach to each of the following matters.

- How often, how long, and where will the group meet?
  (1) Will it begin and end promptly? How much leeway will members feel comfortable allowing?
  (2) If meeting in members' homes, will the location rotate or is it easier routinely to find the same place? Would everyone be more comfortable in a "neutral" place; for example, the church library? In any case, if refreshments are to be served (and maybe they will not be), how will members share that responsibility?
- How will group members share leadership responsibilities? It is strongly urged that the group rotate leadership among members, so that all feel a sense of ownership for what happens in the group; but there may be different ways to handle this. Will only one person provide leadership for each meeting, with that one (1) guiding the *lectio* and selecting the scripture, (2) bringing refreshments, and (3) taking responsibility to insure that these tasks are assigned for the next meeting? Or will persons share each of these tasks on a separate rotation? Will these tasks be assigned semipermanently, say for six meetings at a time and then rotate?
- When may new members join the group? If the group decides to accept new members at any time, it may be difficult to establish a sense of shared group identity and trust. On the other hand, if the

group *never* accepts new members, it may grow stale and ingrown. What procedure would the members like to follow with regard to accepting new members?

- How long is the initial commitment that members make to one another and the group? After about four meetings, set aside time for special discussion about how the group is going and whether the group needs to make any modifications in covenant items or group practices. However, establish a basic time of initial commitment at the first meeting. The initial commitment should not exceed one year nor be less than three months. After that time, the group might plan a full meeting given to evaluation of the process, to celebration of successes, and to acknowledgment of difficulties. Group members may wish to terminate the group, or perhaps some will leave and others stay and find new members to join. If the group continues, decide what form it will take and how long the next period of commitment will be.

- Is each member of the group willing to commit to pray for the others between meetings? Including regular prayer for one another in the covenant will greatly enrich the common life of the group.

Ideally, the members will discuss all these issues, at least briefly, during the first meeting and come to a consensus about methods of operation by the end of that meeting. It may help to ask one member to record and write up a summary of the agreement and give everyone a copy. Remember that the objective of developing a covenant is to help shape group life. As such, it is an early means of practicing the theology of *lectio* that life and prayer are mutually influential: We experience "prayer-in-action" in the process of making decisions and working together.

Notice that the intent is not that the group spend the first several meetings arguing about elements of a covenant, thereby effectively using discussion to avoid prayer and reflection on scripture together. On the contrary, an early airing of some of these foundational dynamics will help create a prayerful structure that will enable optimum openness to God and one another.

Sharing Leadership

How does one actually take leadership responsibility in a group *lectio* time? The leadership of a Christian small group differs from our usual ideas about leadership. First, we remember that Jesus taught us about a form of leadership that involves *serving* others:

> But Jesus called them to him and said, "You know that the rulers of the Gentiles lord it over them, and their great ones are tyrants over them. It will not be so among you; but whoever wishes to be great among you must be your servant."
>
> —Matthew 20:25-26

Thus for us, the marks of a good leader are not so much expertise and power as willingness to be oneself and to be open to God's spirit. The small group leader stands alongside, not above, helping each member discover for him- or herself where God is leading. Also in a small group, the members grow in Christ primarily through interaction and discovery, rather than through instruction and advice. As we saw in chapter 2 on community life, each member of the group has an essential contribution. The leader's primary goal is to facilitate the full contribution of members during the session. Given the heart and rhythm of *lectio*, one of the main ways the leader does this is by helping the group stay faithful to the disciplines on which it has agreed in its covenant. Beyond that, the primary tasks of leadership in a *lectio* group are four:

❶ Pray
❷ Prepare
❸ Guide
❹ Care

Pray

Prayer undergirds and strengthens the leader and the group. It is especially important for a) wisdom and sensitivity to the whisperings of the Spirit as the group listens and speaks; b) personal openness to God and to each group member; c) each member and the group as a whole between and before meetings; and d) anything else you feel is needed.

The leader's work is lightened when set in the context of personal prayer.

Prepare

Preparation for group *lectio* is relatively simple, but it does include

1) Anticipating and scheduling time for various components of the meeting. For example, if there is to be open sharing at the beginning or end of the meeting, approximately how much time will be set aside for that? What is the minimum time needed for the full *lectio* process? How long is the babysitter available? If refreshments are available, when should the group adjourn to a less formal mode?

2) Praying over and reviewing the *lectio* process until it becomes completely familiar. The leader might do this by practicing a solitary *lectio* on the proposed passage ahead of time.

3) Seeking others' help as appropriate. For example, you might let others know ahead of time if you plan to ask them to read.

Before the meeting, it is the leader's responsibility to see that the chairs are in a circle, so that everyone is fully included physically. And don't forget to bring either your Bible with your marked selection or a typed copy of the passage to hand to other readers.

Take time at the beginning to relax yourself and others—physically as well as mentally and emotionally—realizing that at each gathering all of us need some time to make the transition from our busy lives into this privileged time of meeting God. Finally, remember that God is in your midst as the group gathers together.

Guide

Giving guidance is the task of facilitating the flow of the *lectio* time. The following are some points the leader will want to keep in mind.

1) It may be helpful to obtain a watch that tells exactly when two or three minutes have passed to alleviate any anxiety about the length of time for silence.

2) During sharing, the leader may have to gently interrupt participants to ask them to stay with the given *lectio* structure. Be prepared to do this without aggression or anger but with firmness
and confidence in the process.

3) Always honor each person's right to pass at any time; never force
anyone to share.

4) At each stage, you will want to repeat the instructions for that
stage briefly, as set out in chapter 1, thus setting a framework of
safety and comfort in which all participants can relax.

5) As leader, you may wish to take a particularly supportive role in
response to the group members' contributions—not a lengthy,
formal response but rather an affirming sound or a thank-you to
each member for sharing.

Do the best you can, and be flexible. Remember, God is the main
guide for your group at every moment.

Care

Caring is the task of attending thoughtfully and fully to each and every
member of the group as shown by sensitive listening and brief responses. Just before the meeting, it may help you to hold each member in your heart and up to God imaginatively, specifically praying that
each may find his or her personal good in this meeting.

Caring also means responding to the needs of a particular situation or moment. For instance in the early meetings, if the group members do not know one another, the leader needs to take time for
introductions and the sharing of names. Similarly, if someone begins
coughing violently or there is a loud noise outside, there is nothing
wrong with interrupting the regular process to acknowledge whatever
is going on. Your best gift of caring is to bring yourself as you are to
the group and to be natural.

Obviously all members of the group will share these "leadership" tasks, but they are the special responsibility and opportunity of
the one who is leading the *lectio*.

Summary

The foundational principle of *lectio* groups is openness to the ongoing conversion of God's spirit and attentive expectancy to the creative Christ to whom we belong. This is easier said than done, and attention to a few basic matters can be a big help.

If you feel the desire to begin a *lectio* group, trust that God has given you that desire and be enthusiastic in your contacts. A group prospers when it begins with a full and frank discussion of how members will conduct themselves. Gain agreement on basic format and procedures and commit to one another that each will assume responsibility for the life of the group. Be aware that mutual leadership is not so much a matter of expertise as it is of loving concern, of prayer, and of supporting one another in everything. May this practice empower you!

4 Passages to Pray

ectio texts can be chosen from any reflective source, even those not in scripture. However, this approach emphasizes scripture as a privileged place of meeting God. Even so, the Bible itself contains many different types of literature, some of which are more suitable and edifying for devotional purposes than others. As a group or individual becomes more and more familiar with the heart and rhythm of *lectio*, it will become the case that *any* text—or indeed any event—can become a place for meeting the living God. In the meantime, it only makes sense to start with those passages that are most helpful and easily accessible for our purpose.

Given the particular focus of our group *lectio* mode, the first ingredient in selecting fruitful texts is to choose ones from the Gospels or the Psalms that have strong action verbs or concrete images. Images such as planting seed, touching a hem, or searching for a lost coin are vivid ways of thinking about God's presence. For example, an excellent text is Luke 5:4-7, which tells about the fishermen's lowering their nets again for a large catch of fish. Or perhaps you might explore a passage like Psalm 23:2, with its image of God's inviting us to rest in green pastures and beside still waters.

Strong action verbs such as *cry out*, *come*, *call forth*, or *leap* help us appropriate the dynamic quality of God in our midst. Examples might include Psalm 22:1-2, which expresses a sense of being abandoned by God with such words as *crying*, *forsaking*, *groaning*. Or we might choose the vivid image in Mark 10:47-48 where the blind beggar hears and shouts, is ordered to silence, and cries even more loudly.

By and large, it is well to avoid strongly doctrinal or cognitive texts, like some of the New Testament epistles, as well as historical or ritual texts such as Judges or Leviticus. Passages loaded with words like *sin*, *salvation*, or *repent* may block our spontaneous response to God because we think we ought to know what such words mean. For example, group *lectio* on a text like this one from Romans 3:23-24 would probably not be fruitful:

> All have sinned and fall short of the glory of God; they are now
> justified by his grace as a gift, through the redemption that is in
> Christ Jesus.

This passage is central to Bible study and in a teaching context can be quite meaningful, but it is far from optimum for the usual *lectio* group.

At the beginning, groups will find the most helpful material in the Gospels—especially Matthew, Mark, and Luke—and in the Psalms, especially those with strong emotional energy. The purpose of *lectio* is to realize and bring home the essence of basic theological truths; the method of *lectio* is to do so through the means of direct engagement from the heart with the holy spirit of God. These suggested texts help evoke responses and inner dialogue at the level of the heart.

The second major ingredient in selecting an appropriate text for group *lectio* is length. The text may range from one verse to ten verses, containing enough words to give group members some flexibility in selection but not so many words that the whole text cannot be generally held in the mind in full. The goal is to give members an opportunity to choose only one word or a short phrase, not—in this case—to teach a whole lesson. Sometimes one might even choose a portion of a story, rather than the whole thing. It is less important to "get the point" than to make a contact with God that relates to our lives.

For example, one of the more moving texts in the Gospels is that of the paralyzed man brought to Jesus by his friends in Mark 2:1-12. All twelve verses is too long a portion for an effective *lectio* time. Instead, the leader might select only a verse or two that would evoke a strong sense of connection with God. It might be good to select, for example, only verses 1b-2:

> It was reported that he was at home. So many gathered around that there was no longer room for them, not even in front of the door; and he was speaking the word to them.

Or perhaps, one might choose verses 11-12:

> [Jesus said,] "I say to you, stand up, take your mat and go to your home." And he stood up, and immediately took the mat and went out before all of them; so that they were all amazed and glorified God, saying, "We have never seen anything like this!"

The goal of *lectio* is to help us incarnate a way of dialoguing with God about our specific life issues in such a way that transformation can occur through God's work in our midst. Throughout the centuries, Christians have discovered the words of the Bible to be so rich in the vital presence of God that *lectio divina* (*lectio* on scripture) has been the main reflective center for *lectio*. However, when *lectio* functions in our hearts as intended, it begins to predispose us for dialogue with God in reflective engagement with elements other than the Bible. Always, the writings and sayings of "holy" persons have been known to be important supplements to the Bible. And in time, even the events of our lives will initiate the mode of reflective dialogue with God. (See chapter 5.)

The remainder of this chapter consists of sample texts (from the Gospels and other New Testament books, the Hebrew Scriptures, and spiritual classics) that a beginning group might use. When the members gradually gain a feel for the type of texts that work best for them, they will certainly want to branch out beyond these.

Sample Gospel Texts

Matthew 5:13-16a

You are the salt of the earth; but if salt has lost its taste, how can its saltiness be restored? It is no longer good for anything, but is thrown out and trampled underfoot. You are the light of the world. A city built on a hill cannot be hid. No one after lighting a lamp puts it under the bushel basket, but on the lampstand, and it gives light to all in the house. In the same way, let your light shine.

Matthew 11:28-30

Come to me, all you that are weary and are carrying heavy burdens, and I will give you rest. Take my yoke upon you, and learn from me; for I am gentle and humble in heart, and you will find rest for your souls. For my yoke is easy, and my burden is light.

Matthew 13:3b-8

Listen! A sower went out to sow. And as he sowed, some seeds fell on the path, and the birds came and ate them up. Other seeds fell on rocky ground, where they did not have much soil, and they sprang up quickly, since they had no depth of soil. But when the sun rose, they were scorched; and since they had no root, they withered away. Other seeds fell among thorns, and the thorns grew up and choked them. Other seeds fell on good soil and brought forth grain, some a hundredfold, some sixty, some thirty.

Matthew 13:31-33

[Jesus] put before them another parable: "The kingdom of heaven is like a mustard seed that someone took and sowed in his field; it is the smallest of all the seeds, but when it has grown it is the greatest of shrubs and becomes a tree, so that the birds of the air come and make nests in its branches." He told them another parable: "The kingdom of heaven is like yeast that a woman took and mixed in with three measures of flour until all of it was leavened."

Mark 1:35-37

In the morning, while it was still very dark, [Jesus] got up and went out to a deserted place, and there he prayed. And Simon and his companions hunted for him. When they found him, they said to him: "Everyone is searching for you!"

Mark 4:26-28

[Jesus] also said, "The kingdom of God is as if someone would scatter seed on the ground, and would sleep and rise night and day, and the seed would sprout and grow, he does not know how. The earth produces of itself, first the stalk, then the head, then the full grain in the head."

Mark 11:2-4, 7-9

[Jesus said to two of his disciples:] "Go into the village ahead of you, and immediately as you enter it, you will find tied there a colt that has never been ridden; untie it and bring it. If anyone says to you, 'Why are you doing this?' just say this, 'The Lord needs it and will send it back here immediately.'" They went away and found a colt tied near a door. . . . Then they brought the colt to Jesus and threw their cloaks on it; and he sat on it. Many people spread their cloaks on the road, and others spread leafy branches that they had cut in the fields. Then those who went ahead and those who followed were shouting, "Hosanna! Blessed is the one who comes in the name of the Lord!"

Luke 3:10-14

And the crowds asked [John], "What then should we do?" In reply he said to them, "Whoever has two coats must share with anyone who has none; and whoever has food must do likewise." Even tax collectors came to be baptized, and they asked him, 'Teacher, what should we do?" He said to them, "Collect no more than the amount prescribed for you." Soldiers also asked him, "And we, what should we do?" He said to them, "Do not extort money from anyone by threats or false accusation, and be satisfied with your wages." . . . The people were filled with expectation.

Luke 5:4-7

When [Jesus] had finished speaking, he said to Simon, "Put out into the deep water, and let down your nets for a catch." Simon answered, "Master, we have worked all night long but have caught nothing. Yet if you say so, I will let down the nets." When they had done this, they caught so many fish that their nets were beginning to break. So they signaled their partners in the other boat to come and help them. And they came and filled both boats, so that they began to sink.

Luke 7:44b-47

[Jesus said,] "Do you see this woman? I entered your house; you gave me no water for my feet, but she has bathed my feet with her tears and dried them with her hair. You gave me no kiss, but from the time I came in she has not stopped kissing my feet. You did not anoint my head with oil, but she has anointed my feet with ointment. Therefore, I tell you, her sins, which were many, have been forgiven—hence she has shown great love."

Luke 9:1-6

Then Jesus called the twelve together and gave them power and authority over all demons and to cure diseases, and he sent them out to proclaim the kingdom of God and to heal. He said to them, "Take nothing for your journey, no staff, nor bag, nor bread, nor money—not even an extra tunic. Whatever house you enter, stay there, and leave from there. Wherever they do not welcome you, as you are leaving that town, shake the dust off your feet as a testimony against them." They departed and went through the villages, bringing the good news and curing diseases everywhere.

Luke 14:16-21

Someone gave a great dinner and invited many. At the time for the dinner he sent his slave to say to those who had been invited, "Come; for everything is ready now." But they all alike began to make excuses. The first said to him, "I have bought a piece of land, and I must go out and see it; please accept my regrets." Another said, "I have bought five yoke of oxen, and I am going to try them out; please accept my regrets." Another said, "I have just been married, and therefore I cannot come." So the slave returned and reported this to his master.

John 1:35-39

The next day John again was standing with two of his disciples, and as he watched Jesus walk by, he exclaimed, "Look, here is the Lamb of God!" The two disciples heard him say this, and they followed Jesus. When Jesus turned and saw them following, he said to them, "What are you looking for?" They said to him, "Rabbi" (which translated means Teacher) "where are you staying?" He said to them, "Come and see."

John 15:15-16a

I do not call you servants any longer, because the servant does not know what the master is doing; but I have called you friends, because I have made known to you everything that I have heard from my Father. You did not choose me but I chose you. And I appointed you to go and bear fruit, fruit that will last.

Other New Testament Possibilities

Acts 3:4-8
Peter looked intently at [the man lame from birth], as did John, and said, "Look at us." And he fixed his attention on them, expecting to receive something from them. But Peter said, "I have no silver or gold, but what I have I give you; in the name of Jesus Christ of Nazareth, stand up and walk." And he took him by the right hand and raised him up; and immediately his feet and ankles were made strong. Jumping up, he stood and began to walk, and he entered into the temple with them, walking and leaping, and praising God.

Colossians 3:14-16a
Above all clothe yourselves with love, which binds everything together in perfect harmony. And let the peace of Christ rule in your hearts, to which indeed you were called in the one body. And be thankful. Let the word of Christ dwell in you richly.

Philippians 4:5-8
Let your gentleness be known to everyone. The Lord is near. Do not worry about anything, but in everything by prayer and supplication with thanksgiving let your requests be made known to God. And the peace of God, which surpasses all understanding, will guard your hearts and your minds in Christ Jesus.

Sample Texts from the Hebrew Scriptures

Genesis 1:21-22a
So God created the great sea monsters and every living creature that moves, of every kind, with which the waters swarm, and every winged bird of every kind. And God saw that it was good. God blessed them, saying, "Be fruitful."

Genesis 28:11-12, 16
[Jacob] came to a certain place and stayed there for the night, because the sun had set. Taking one of the stones of the place, he put it under his head and lay down in that place. And he dreamed that there was a ladder set up on the earth, the top of it reaching to heaven; and the angels of God were ascending and descending on it. . . . Then Jacob woke from

his sleep and said, "Surely the Lord is in this place—and I did not know it!"

Exodus 15:1-2

Then Moses and the Israelites sang this song to the Lord: "I will sing to the Lord, for [God] has triumphed gloriously; horse and rider he has thrown into the sea. The Lord is my strength and my might, and he has become my salvation; this is my God, and I will praise him, my [ancestor's] God and I will exalt him."

Deuteronomy 30:11-12, 14

Surely, this commandment that I am commanding you today is not too hard for you, nor is it too far away. It is not in heaven, that you should say, "Who will go up to heaven for us, and get it for us so that we may hear it and observe it?". . . No, the word is very near to you; it is in your mouth and in your heart for you to observe.

1 Samuel 3:9

Therefore Eli said to Samuel, "Go, lie down; and if [God] calls you, you shall say, 'Speak, Lord, for your servant is listening.'"

1 Kings 19:11-13

[The word of the Lord came to Elijah:] "Go out and stand on the mountain before the Lord, for the Lord is about to pass by." Now there was a great wind, so strong that it was splitting mountains . . . but the Lord was not in the wind; and after the wind an earthquake, but the Lord was not in the earthquake; and after the earthquake a fire, but the Lord was not in the fire; and after the fire a sound of sheer silence. When Elijah heard it, he wrapped his face in his mantle and went out and stood at the entrance of the cave. Then there came a voice to him that said, "What are you doing here?"

Esther 4:15-17

Then Esther said in reply to Mordecai, "Go, gather all [our people] to be found in Susa, and hold a fast on my behalf, and neither eat nor drink for three days, night or day. I and my maids will also fast as you do. After that I will go to the king, though it is against the law; and if I perish, I perish." Mordecai then went away and did everything as Esther had ordered him.

Psalm 46:10-11

"Be still, and know that I am God! I am exalted among the nations, I am exalted in the earth." The Lord of hosts is with us; the God of Jacob is our refuge.

Psalm 95:6-8a

O come, let us worship and bow down, let us kneel before the Lord our Maker! For he is our God, and we are the people of his pasture and the sheep of his hand. O that today you would listen to [God's] voice! Do not harden your hearts.

Psalm 127:1-2

Unless the Lord builds the house, those who build it labor in vain. Unless the Lord guards the city, the guard keeps watch in vain. It is in vain that you rise up early and go late to rest, eating the bread of anxious toil; for [God] gives sleep to [the] beloved.

Ecclesiastes 11:1-2, 5; 12:1

Send out your bread upon the waters, for after many days you will get it back. Divide your means seven ways, or even eight, for you do not know what . . . may happen on earth. . . . Just as you do not know how the breath comes to the bones in the mother's womb, so you do not know the work of God, who makes everything. . . . Remember your creator.

Song of Solomon 2:10-13

My beloved speaks and says to me: "Arise my love, my fair one, and come away; for now the winter is past, the rain is over and gone. The flowers appear on the earth; the time of singing has come, and the voice of the turtledove is heard in our land. The fig tree puts forth its figs, and the vines are in blossom; they give forth fragrance. Arise, my love, my fair one, and come away [with me].

Isaiah 55:10-12a

For as the rain and the snow come down from heaven, and do not return there until they have watered the earth, making it bring forth and sprout, giving seed to the sower and bread to the eater, so shall my word be that goes out from my mouth; it shall not return to me empty, but it shall accomplish that which I purpose and succeed in the thing for which I sent it. For you shall go out in joy and be led back in peace.

Ezekiel 36:26-27a

A new heart I will give you, and a new spirit I will put within you; and

I will remove from your body the heart of stone and give you a heart of flesh. I will put my spirit within you.

Hosea 2:14-15a

Therefore, I will now allure her, and bring her into the wilderness, and speak tenderly to her. From there I will give her her vineyards, and make the Valley of Achor a door of hope. There she shall respond as in the days of her youth.

Joel 2:28-29

Then afterward I will pour out my spirit on all flesh; your sons and your daughters shall prophesy, your old men shall dream dreams, and your young men shall see visions. Even on the male and female slaves, in those days, I will pour out my spirit.

Zephaniah 3:17

The Lord, your God, is in your midst, a warrior who gives victory; [God] will rejoice over you with gladness, [God] will renew you in . . . love and . . . exult over you with loud singing.

Zechariah 2:4-5, 10

[The angel] said, "Run, say to that young man: 'Jerusalem shall be inhabited like villages without walls, because of the multitude of people and animals in it. For I will be a wall of fire all around it,' says the Lord, 'and I will be the glory within it. . . . Sing and rejoice, O daughter of Zion! For lo, I will come and dwell in your midst.'"

Malachi 3:7b, 10

"Return to me, and I will return to you," says the Lord of hosts. But you say, "How shall we return?" . . . "Bring the full tithe into the storehouse, that there may be food in my house, and thus put me to the test," says the Lord of hosts; "see if I will not open the windows of heaven for you and pour down for you an overflowing blessing."

Sirach 1:1-4

All wisdom is from the Lord, and with [God] it remains forever. The sands of the sea, the drops of rain, and the days of eternity—who can count them? The height of heaven, the breadth of the earth, the abyss, and wisdom—who can search them out? Wisdom was created before all other things, and prudent understanding from eternity.

Sample Texts from Spiritual Classics

Saint Augustine of Hippo (A.D. 354–430, Egypt)
Confessions: I shall know you, my knower, I shall know you "even as I am known." Power of my soul, enter into it and fit it for yourself, so that you may have it and hold it "without spot or wrinkle." This is my hope. (Book 10, Chapter 1, 229; New York: Image Books, 1960)

Saint Benedict of Nursia (ca. 480–547, Italy)
Rule: Be chaste, temperate, and merciful. . . . Let mercy triumph over judgment so that [you] too may win mercy. . . . Use prudence and avoid extremes; otherwise by rubbing too hard to remove the rust, [you] may break the vessel. (64:9-12; Collegeville, MN: The Liturgical Press, 1982)

Saint Bernard of Clairvaux (A.D. 1090–1153, France)
On Loving God: [Our] frequent needs oblige [us] to invoke God more often and approach God more frequently. This intimacy moves us to taste and discover how sweet the Lord is. Tasting God's sweetness entices [us] more to pure love than does the urgency of our own needs. (IX: 26; Washington D. C.: Cistercian Publications CF13, 1974)

Hildegard of Bingen (A.D. 1098–1179, Germany)
Scivias (or "Know the Ways"): For the soul passes through the body just as sap passes through a tree. What does this mean? It is through the sap that a tree is green, produces flowers, and then fruit. And how does the fruit come to maturity? By the mildness of the air. The sun warms it, the rain waters it, and it is perfected by the mildness of the air. What is the significance of this? The mercy of the grace of God will make a person bright as the sun, the breath of the Holy Spirit will water the person just as the rain, and thus discretion will lead the person to the perfection of good fruits just like the mildness of the air does for the tree. (Vision Four: 25, 55; Bear & Co., 1986)

Anonymous (fourteenth-century, England)
The Cloud of Unknowing: And so diligently persevere [in this prayer] until you feel joy in it. For in the beginning it is usual to feel nothing but a kind of darkness about your mind, or as it were, a *cloud of unknowing*. You will seem to know nothing and to feel nothing except a naked intent toward God in the depths of your being. . . . Learn to be at home in this darkness. Return to it as often as you can, letting your spirit cry out

to [God] whom you love. (Chapter 3, 48–9; New York: Image Books, 1973)

Julian(a) of Norwich (ca. 1343–ca. 1416, England)
Showings (Long Text): And then I saw that only pain blames and punishes, and our courteous Lord comforts and succours, and always he is kindly disposed to the soul, loving and longing to bring us to his bliss. (Chapter 51, 271; New York: Paulist Press, 1978)

Brother Lawrence of the Resurrection (A.D. 1611–91, France)
The Practice of the Presence of God: Comfort yourself with thoughts of [God] as often as you can. Lift up your heart to [God] sometimes when you are at meals or in society; the least little remembrance will always be pleasing to [God]. There is no need to cry very loudly, for [God] is nearer to us than we think. (Fourth Letter, 68; Springfield, IL: Templegate, 1974)

Jean-Pierre de Caussade (A.D. 1675–1751, France)
The Sacrament of the Present Moment: The present moment holds infinite riches beyond your wildest dreams but you will only enjoy them to the extent of your faith and love. The more a soul loves, the more it longs, the more it hopes, the more it finds. The will of God is manifest in each moment, an immense ocean which the heart only fathoms in so far as it overflows with faith, trust, and love. (Chapter 9, 62; San Francisco: Harper & Row, 1981)

Thomas Kelly (1893–1941, United States of America)
A Testament of Devotion: The outer distractions of our interests reflect an inner lack of integration of our own lives. We are trying to be several selves at once, without all our selves being organized by a single, mastering Life within us. ("The Simplification of Life," 114; New York: Harper & Brothers Publishers, 1941)

Evelyn Underhill (1875–1941, England)
Abba: Thy Kingdom come! We open our gates to the Perfect, and entreat its transfiguring presence; redeeming our. . . disharmonies. We face the awful contrast between the Actual and the Real, and acknowledge our need of deliverance. . . . The Kingdom is the serenity of God already enfolding us, and seeking to penetrate and redeem the whole of this created order. (Chapter IV, 28–29; Cincinnati, OH: Forward Movement Publications, 1940)

5 Praying Our Lives

hapter 4 offered examples of how to select *lectio* texts primarily from scripture but also from spiritual classics. That chapter suggested that we may find appropriate texts for *lectio* in reflective engagement with many sources. The practice of praying the scriptures is intended to form us in spiritual growth with the aim of deepened receptivity to God's life in our innermost being. *Lectio divina* gradually enables us to discover that even the ordinary events of our lives may serve as "texts" for engagement with God. This chapter explores our "*lectio* on life," the use of life experiences as *lectio* texts. After presenting the basic concept, I propose a specific method and give a group example.

Lectio as a New Way of Seeing

As a personal rhythm of *lectio* experience begins to emerge, group members will begin subtly to sense a new kind of awareness. Members come to the group meeting with a certain expectancy—or maybe even an almost superstitious awe—based on the aggregate of past experiences. How astonishing it is to discover, time after time, that God actually meets us in this process! How amazing it is that, even when we don't exactly know what our needs are, as we settle down into the quiet reflection of group *lectio*, we receive something of strength or hope for our life! How gracious that this apparently new, yet completely ordinary, element is so consistently added to our situations when we offer them to God!

God Found in Life as in Scripture

We return again and again to the recognition that *lectio* is about the intersection of human and divine, or prayer and life. In *lectio*, we experience these "opposites" as somehow unified, and we receive guidance for the next best step we can take to express this unity in our situation. *Lectio* does not force us to choose between intimacy with God and an active life in the world but instead enables us to integrate those two important poles of human experience.

Lectio does not allow us to refuse or ignore difficulties in our particular settings; rather it invites us to offer them to God for transformation. We begin to gain a sense that God is teaching us exactly what we need to be and do at this moment within the context of our given circumstances and experiences. So often we may have felt that we could be good and holy if only we did not have to deal with young adolescents or old parents! If only we did not have to cope with that drunken boss, we could really get our act together. If only we were not so crippled by childhood abuse that we suffer continuously from the urge to eat compulsively, then we could really be something special. If only, if only! And yet in *lectio*—and especially *lectio* on life—we discover with amazement that God is calling us to love and serve and be embraced just where we are!

Lectio teaches us that it is misguided to believe that God cannot understand the complexities or earthiness of our life issues; rather, every actual life situation has a prayerful invitation when we are attentive. Jesus' encounters with two non-Jews in whom Jesus is amazed to find God already at work suggests this possibility. It is delightful to imagine Jesus himself teaching us these lessons of *lectio* on life, finding himself meeting the Father in the most unexpected places!

The Syro-Phoenician woman whose daughter is ill is not put off by Jesus' rebuke that food meant for the children should not be given to dogs; instead she bravely responds that even the dogs receive table scraps! And Jesus is delighted, knowing he has encountered God unexpectedly in this saucy but believing woman, and he sends her home assured that her daughter will be well. (See Matt. 15:21-28.)

The incident with the Roman centurion whose slave is sick is similar; Jesus is moved when he encounters such simple faith:

> But when [Jesus] was not far from the house, the centurion sent friends to say to him, "Lord, do not trouble yourself, for I am not worthy to have you come under my roof; therefore I did not presume to come to you. But only speak the word, and let my servant be healed."
>
> —Luke 7:6-7

Again, Jesus is amazed; he is in wonder at the unexpected encounter with God's life moving in this foreigner; and again he lets his power go forth in cooperation with that which is already present. Such images are a bit fanciful, but they highlight nuances of earthly life taught us in our Lord's incarnation.

Lectio invites us to change our way of seeing things, to allow ourselves to be surprised by encounters with God in unlikely places. We are no longer stuck alone in the middle of disaster or lifted far above the fray. We are still in the middle of our troubles; but now we have options, possibilities beyond our imagining, because we are not alone. We begin to look for God in Christ in every event, encounter, moment. We begin to sense the tangible yet hidden presence of the kingdom that, although not yet fulfilled, is somehow already here.

What began as a willingness to believe that we might find the living God in scripture extends to a willingness to believe that we might find the living God in creation also. God is Creator; does not the very structure of the world somehow reveal the mark—the presence—of the Artist? Maybe it is true as C. S. Lewis observes that "the world is crowded with [God]. . . . The real labour is to remember, to attend. In fact, to come awake. Still more, to remain awake"![3] If so, *lectio* is a marvelous way to "read" life as well as scripture with the same result of a transforming encounter with God.

We may practice *lectio* using life events as texts as well as scripture! Just as we receive the pages of scripture to read, mark, learn, and inwardly digest; so can we receive each day's incidents for reflection. Just as we encounter Christ in scripture with a word of strength and hope, so may we encounter Christ in life situations with a transforming word. The deep intention of *lectio* is a transfer of its lessons from book to life. We may wish to explore this possibility directly by the practice of *lectio* on life situations themselves, as well as to reap the natural fruits that come from ongoing *lectio divina*.

Life is not a substitute for scripture (or vice versa), and it is well to sustain devotional reflection on scripture whether or not you deliberately add devotional reflection on life. Both exercises express and incarnate a way of seeing/hearing that involves a new capacity to respond to God in one's midst, wherever one finds oneself.

Lectio on life is based on the conviction that God is present in every single event, encounter, and thought. We find urgent invitation to *lectio* on life in the pivotal experience of the Hebrews' wandering the desert, forced by thirst to cry out their pain: "Is the Lord among us or not?" (Ex. 17:7). And significantly, God answers this cry with the generous response of living water flowing forth from the "rock" of daily life experience. Is God among us or not? In every tiny moment and obscure place, God is waiting to surprise and delight us. When we see and hear, our lives are transformed; we have new choices; and we become cocreators in the coming of God's kingdom.

Holding Life and Prayer in Tension

All Christian spiritual practices combine prayer and life to some extent, but this connection is a particularly marked characteristic of *lectio* and its sources. Every Christian spiritual practice attracts those who find it an especially fruitful way to God; the diversity in spiritual practice simply reflects the diversity in temperament, timing, need. The prayer way of *lectio* is definitely on the kataphatic, or physical, end of the spectrum: It is a way of images and engagement with the many, although it also involves the apophatic, or imageless, side—*in rhythmic interchange* with images. Apophatic prayer, or prayer that seeks to rest in God with no images and no thoughts, is often taught today as the best way to "listen" to God in prayer. But an equally respected tradition is the practice of kataphatic prayer—using images and thoughts, especially from scripture, as a means to be attentive to God's guidance. All prayer rests in the unknowable and unnameable God. However, *lectio* does not aim to stay in the wordless and imageless dimension, as so many modern spiritual exercises do. Rather it always draws us back into life experience as an essential part of the prayer; its goal is always the growing integration of prayer into life and of life into prayer.

Because of *lectio*'s earthiness, some may think that it is not mystical. Yet other participants will initially find it far too mysterious and formless for their liking, especially if they are predisposed to the cut-and-dried, precise, and definitive modes of modern technical and engineering thought (which has affected a large segment of the modern church, where there is a sense that God can be definitively known). Yet *lectio* equally refuses to be confined by the "imaged" end of the prayer continuum. It knows a God whose ways are not our ways and about whom all language is only an approximation.

When *lectio* urges us to consider that God has a particular and unique word for each one of us, we must not imagine that we will hear a voice speaking in our ear, saying, "Turn right at the next intersection"! The conviction that God cares about us and is so involved in our lives as to be present in response to our call does not mean that we have reduced God to our size. But it does mean that a power greater than ourselves can help us, if we are willing to consider the possibility in terms we do not necessarily understand and certainly do not control. Such an approach is similar to the modern spiritual phenomenon of twelve-step groups based on Alcoholics Anonymous's insight that all of us contain inner chambers where we do not yet trust a power greater than ourselves. In certain secret compartments, all of us share the pain of the man who cries, "I believe; help my unbelief!" (Mark 9:24).

One of human life's most pressing issues has to do with the experience of great trials that seem to contradict the gifts of a loving God. These trials may be so personal and so close that we think of them as trivial compared to what others suffer and yet they are, for us, very difficult to bear. Trials might involve watching one's early adult-age children make poor choices. We might be suffering from a chronic physical handicap or disease; we may have to relate to a dishonest or severely demanding boss or to a gossipy and rude next-door neighbor. Trials might involve the slow recovery of childhood memories of abuse, trusting that healing will come in time or gathering courage to leave a present abusive situation. Some might be struggling to learn to love honestly when everything in their background teaches them to hate or an unexpected loss brings bitterness. Trials might involve caring for an ungrateful parent or a mentally challenged child or the personal agony of working in a humiliating corporate environment.

When we live with our eyes wide open to the actual situations in our environment, it is often difficult to believe in the call that each of us has to holiness. Yet each of us has such a call; and at some level, we know it. There is a deep, maybe hidden, inner longing to share in God's life, to know ourselves infinitely precious, to be embraced in the loving union of absolute wordless understanding with the Great Other. At some level of ourselves, each of us can get in touch with this call when we are quiet. And here God meets us, just as Christ met Matthew the "sinner" and went to dinner with him, responding generously to those who know their need. (Read Matt. 9:9-13).

Yet it is often painful to know our need, to believe in the irresistibly attractive invitation of God to be the beloved. Like touching one's hand to a hot fire, the pain comes from recognizing the invitation while acknowledging the great distance between our weary and often irritable daily round and the mysterious grace God offers.

We usually do what we can to hide from one side or the other of this double truth. We close our eyes to the reality and live in an interior fantasy world, telling ourselves that the present suffering is only temporary illusion. Or we close our ears to the call and embrace of God, telling ourselves that if God really were calling us to such a state, real life would be different. We may think it better to believe in no God than to suffer the tension between what we long for and what we have.

The process of *lectio* on life invites us to live actively into both sides of this double truth: both the reality of the hard trials we must endure and the reality of our personal call to holiness. When we do this, we somehow participate in the blossoming forth of God's kingdom for which we daily pray. God apparently awaits and then uses our willingness to be stretched between these apparent contradictions in order to do the work in the world, which is its fulfillment. On reflection, we realize that Christ our Lord did just this work of living into both sides of the double truth, as did his mother. We also are invited to this work. This formative perspective of *lectio* integrates life and prayer.

Group Practice of *Lectio* on Life

With this background, we turn to the practical question of how to practice *lectio* on life. What specific method can help us more fully integrate our prayer and our life, our trials and our call? How do we begin to express this perspective and this willingness in our actual life settings? How do we read the "texts" of life in *lectio*? Here we explore one method, using our continuing group example.

The pattern of *lectio* on life follows that of basic *lectio*. The outline of our method follows:

- Prepare
- Hear the word.
  Review recent life events and select a single incident for reflection.
- How is your life touched?
  Review the incident mentally and emotionally as it happened, then be receptive to a phrase or image that seems to be given in relation to it.
- Is there an invitation here?
  Offer the incident and your reflections back to God, then rest and be responsive to an invitation that might come.
- Pray

As with *lectio divina*, you may practice *lectio* on life alone or in a group. In group practice, *lectio* on life may require more time than that required for *lectio divina*. *Lectio* on life involves more directive and explicit guidance, as well as generally requires a deeper level of intimacy. The group practice is as follows:

Prepare

The group members gather and sit in a circle. The leader invites the group to begin with a recollection process: each takes a comfortable but alert position, closing eyes and concentrating on breath. Use exhalations to release tension and preoccupations; use inhalations to receive God's presence here and now. The group members gradually let their thoughts die away, seeking to be fully open to this moment.

Example

The group from Immanuel Church has been meeting for nine months and has decided to try a *lectio* on life this time. The meeting is at the home of Mary and Bill, and Charles is the leader. As before, all six gather and settle food, children, and themselves. The group has asked the sitter to stay about half an hour longer this time; they expect the *lectio* on life practice to take somewhat longer than usual.

Charles officially convenes the group and leads the members in a time of preparatory quieting, reminding everyone to sit comfortably, close eyes, and center with breath for several quiet minutes.

**Stage One:
Hear the Word**

The leader invites the members, still with their eyes closed, to review mentally the events of the last few days or week, gently and attentively turning the "pages" of their recent life experiences. The aim is simply to recall what happened day by day or hour by hour. As memorable moments come to mind, gradually let each memory pass through your awareness. After a time, perhaps one event or situation seems to recur again and again in your thoughts. Perhaps one moment seems especially to seek greater attention and reflection.

Each member takes time to decide on one particular incident and then holds it easily in the mind. After a few moments, the leader brings the silence to a close and invites the members one by one to state the approximate time of day when his or her chosen incident occurred. Each one states a time and that is all.

Example

Charles speaks, encouraging group members to think over events of the past several days, letting each situation flow through the mind and finally allowing one particular incident to come to the fore. After two minutes of silence, he asks each person to pass or to share, simply speaking aloud the approximate time of day when the remembered incident occurred. Charles begins by saying, "9 A.M." Jim says, "2 P.M." Ann responds, "I have one incident at 12:30 and one at 6 A.M.; how do I choose?" Charles smiles and replies, "It doesn't matter; either will do. Just go with one of them." Ann decides "12:30." Sharon says, "10 A.M." Bill speaks, "About 6 P.M." Mary states, "I'm not sure—about two o'clock, I think."

Stage Two: How is my life touched?	The leader now invites the group to return in thought to the chosen incident, this time exploring the question, "How is my life touched?"— understanding now that the word *touch* means

particularly *touched by God in Christ*. The leader begins by asking members mentally to review the physical happening of the incident, to recreate it vividly and sequentially in their minds, recalling colors, shapes, textures, smells, sounds, and the like. Give about two minutes of silence for this exercise.

Asking that members continue to keep their eyes closed, the leader encourages them now to recall the incident emotionally, looking especially for the places where they experience the strongest emotional energy (positive or negative) and any moments of noticeable energy shift. Give about a minute of silence to this task.

Now the leader invites the members to set aside the specific incident for a moment, letting their minds be blank if possible. This setting aside of the memory creates an expectant and receptive interior space into which a word of blessing or consecration is invited. So, with a free mind, each person allows a phrase or image that seems somehow related to his or her incident to surface in consciousness. The phrase or image may be from scripture—a psalm phrase or a Gospel incident, for example—or a favorite hymn. The person does not need to understand the reason why the image emerges or its connection to the incident. Each one just lets some phrase or image come into awareness. Give about two minutes of silence to this task.

Finally, the leader reminds the participants that the image or phrase they have received is a kind of blessing or consecration of the incident, a sign of Christ's presence in it. The leader now invites each to share briefly only the phrase or image received. In just a sentence or two, each person may describe the phrase or image of blessing discovered (not their life incident), beginning with the words *I hear*, *I see*, or *I sense*. As before, it is always permissible to pass.

Example

Charles asks the group members to close their eyes and relax, now mentally recalling the selected incident in some detail, trying to recreate sensorially exactly what happened, remembering sights, sounds, smells—the sequence of events. After about a minute, Bill starts to say, "It was last Thursday, . . ." but Charles quickly says, "We don't share the specifics out loud now, Bill; just stay with your memories in silence for now." At the end of two minutes, Charles suggests that all continue with their eyes closed while he gives a bit more guidance.

Charles encourages each one to continue reflecting on the specific incident, going over it again in terms of the feelings during the occurrence. He asks participants to let the feelings flow in sequence as they did then, noticing particularly any sharp rise or fall in energy and pondering what was going on when such energy shifts occurred. Charles asks continued silence for this further reflection.

After another two minutes, Charles asks everyone to relax, setting aside all thought and being open to any image or phrase that comes. It might be a person (Abraham or Paul) or a phrase ("Oh, God, help") or maybe a favorite image from a book (Fiver's vision in *Watership Down*) or a phrase from a hymn ("What a friend we have!"). All wait quietly, ready to receive some phrase or image somehow related to the incident they have been pondering. When received, each person holds the image or phrase quietly in mind.

Charles gives about two minutes of silence for this task and then encourages everyone to understand the image or phrase as a sign of Christ's presence in the incident. He then invites members to share just the image or phrase received.

There are several seconds more of silence. Finally, Sharon says, "What I see is not from scripture; it's Brother Lawrence with his arms up to his elbows in soapy dishwater!"

Jim voices his image, "I see Jesus in the wilderness with Satan; I don't know how that can be a blessing."

Mary speaks, "I hear the verse from Psalm 42: 'My soul longs for you like the deer for streams of water.'"

Bill says, "You all know the scripture better than I do. I see Huckleberry Finn, sitting on the edge of a river with bare feet dangling in the water and a piece of straw hanging out his mouth. Now that's a blessing!"

Ann responds by saying, "This shifting around is pretty confusing to me. I pass."

Charles says, "I see Jacob waking up and realizing that God was in this spot where he slept, and he had not known it."

**Stage Three:
Is there an invitation here?**

When all have shared or passed, the leader again asks the members to center themselves, remembering Christ's active presence in their midst and resting in that presence. Then the leader asks them to close their eyes again and bring back to mind both their life incident and the image or phrase associated with it. The leader asks that they place, in their imagination, both the incident and their reflections into an offering plate and to lift the plate up to God, placing on top of the offering the image or phrase that came to bless it. Each one offers to God everything connected with this incident—any insight, any confusion or pain, any unresolved feelings—all are offered back to God now. You offer what was done, what was not done, what might be done—giving all back to the Giver of all things. If anyone needs to hold part back, that is all right; but each tries to give everything connected with the incident and reflection back to God. It might help to exhale deeply, perhaps even loudly, and physically let it out. Give about one minute of silence for this.

After completing this action of offering, the leader invites group members to rest as peacefully as possible in God's all-embracing presence, content for a time to be with God without comment. Let this silence last about one minute.

Finally the leader encourages each person to be receptive to any invitation or encouragement that may seem to be given in relation to all that has been pondered here. Does the incident, after reflection, suggest an invitation to do or be something in the next few days? Or does the image or phrase that surfaced carry with it an invitation? Perhaps in the offering to God some sudden insight emerged. Or possibly in the silence and rest, a word of encouragement or hope seemed to appear. Taken together, does there seem to be an invitation to do or be something in the next few days? Members ponder these questions for about two or three minutes silently, and then the leader asks everyone to share his or her invitation or to pass. Sharing may be lengthier this time, and each one pays particular attention to the sharing of the person on his or her right.

Example

Charles draws the group back into silence again, asking that all bring to mind both their incident and the image or phrase that blessed it. They are to imaginatively place everything in an offering plate and lift it up to God. The image or phrase settles imaginatively on top of the offered incident—like a sign of blessing, a sign of Christ's presence in the incident. Then they hand all over to God. Charles encourages members to make a loud sigh of exhalation to express their offering, as if saying, "Here, God, take it now!" After that, he tells them that they will have a time of sitting quietly in silence, resting in God. Charles gives a total of about two minutes for both elements, the offering and the resting.

After the two minutes have elapsed, Charles asks the members to stay in inner silence a little longer, especially receptive now to any invitation that may be given in connection with their *lectio* on life. In the quiet, does any invitation come to do or be something in the next few days? Might that invitation be expressed in words? Charles gives another two minutes' silence for this request.

Drawing the silence to a close, Charles asks the group members to share now, at more length if they wish, about what each one feels invited to do or be as a result of this reflection. Anyone may pass, but those who wish may state their invitation aloud.

Bill says, "Boy, it's pretty clear to me that I'm being invited to lay back a little in the next few days, just to relax and get my bare feet in the water, so to speak! If Mary's game, maybe I'll take Wednesday off and drive up into the mountains!"

Mary responds, "I'd love to, Bill. Maybe we can find a running stream with a deer beside it! I think my invitation is to be with God a little more; so possibly if we go up, we could each kind of wander on our own and then come back together to share a little of what we discovered! I'm due for a little time off."

After a moment, Ann says irritably, "The incident I remember was a terrific fight I had with my mother on the phone last week. And it upsets me a lot to remember it. She never listens to me, and she's always putting me down; I can never win with her. And I don't know why you made me remember it when it brings up so much pain for me!"

Sharon reaches out and squeezes Ann's hand. After a moment Sharon says, "Some days I feel so depressed, and my incident involved such a day. But the image of Brother Lawrence's finding God in the soapsuds made me laugh inside, and I began to feel an invitation to find God in all that the day brings—both good and bad. I can't imagine how to find God in depression, but this week I plan to look."

Jim starts to say something, then stops and is silent for a few seconds. Then he speaks, "There is something funny about this whole process for me. You all know that I have stuck with it only because I love you, and I've wanted our group to continue meeting. But it's weird. I mean, I used to feel quite certain about things; everything about my faith was black and white. And now so much seems fuzzy. And yet somehow, that's not bad! There is a peace in my heart that I never felt when everything was so clear intellectually. In the past, even with my faith in God, I still felt responsible for everything; I felt I had to make things happen. But now I feel I can occasionally trust things to God . . . not all the time, mind you, but now and then! And I see why the image of Jesus with Satan is really a blessing to me: In response to Satan's temptations, Jesus keeps saying, 'I place myself under God the Father's will and power; no matter how gifted I am, the main thing I do is to put God first above all.' And I see that way of being as an invitation to me in my life now."

Charles says, "Sometimes I feel like Rip Van Winkle just waking up from a long sleep. Everything around me seems so alive, so vivid these days! On my way to work one day last week, it was as if suddenly I woke up and really heard the birdsong and saw the marvelous color of the autumn leaves and smelled the fresh, crisp air, . . . and it was all so wonderful, I felt speechless! Old Jacob really had it pegged: 'God is in this place, and I did not know it!'

Stage Four: Pray

When all members have shared or passed, the leader asks each person to pray for the person on his/her right hand, praying for resources to do or be what has been sensed as invitation. The praying moves around the circle to the left so that the one prayed for has time to rest in that prayer. Everyone is asked to pray, though anyone may choose to pray silently. At the end of each prayer, the one praying says "Amen," and the group repeats it. When all have prayed, persons do not get up immediately but allow a few easy moments for the transition back to ordinary life interactions.

Example

Charles continues, "Each of us will pray for the person on the right, asking God to enable our response to this invitation. We all join in the amen each time. I'll begin.

"God, I do pray for my sister Mary and for her deep heartfelt longing for you. I ask you to help her set aside some time for you in the next week and to know that she is as loved and cared for by you as any creature of the forest. Amen." All respond amen.

Jim prays, "God, you know how much I love this guy, and how much of an inspiration his simple faith is for me. I think he's plenty awake, but I know he longs for more. I pray you'll keep giving him more and more of yourself and help him keep sharing that with us. Amen." All respond amen.

Ann says, "I'll pray silently." She takes Jim's hand in both of hers and bows her head for a minute or so. Then she says "Amen," and everyone responds amen. Jim looks moved and continues to hold Ann's hands.

Sharon prays, "Our God, be with my friend Ann. I know how hard she struggles sometimes to keep her head above water and how much she has to overcome. Do embrace her in her pain; do bring her healing. Amen." All respond amen.

Bill prays, "Heavenly Father, I ask you to continue blessing our sister Sharon. She is such a source of warm caring to us, that I pray you will help her receive in abundance both our caring for her and your care for her. Especially be with her the next time she feels depressed and let her know you are there. Amen." All respond amen.

Mary prays, "Father/Mother God, how much I thank you for my husband, Bill, and for his growing willingness to play with you and me and the kids. I pray especially that you will tickle his feet with water and warm his back with sun and generally be so inviting to him that he delights to set aside time for you this week. Amen." All respond amen.

The group members look up and smile shyly at one another, stretch a bit, touch one another briefly, and gradually move out toward the family room for supper.

Summary

The description and examples here have presented a means of using our life situations as "text" for *lectio* reflection in a group process. The process may seem a bit cumbersome at first, as is any new discipline, such as tennis or playing the piano. Gradually the group will become accustomed to the pattern, and it will flow more easily. To aid the flow in early practice sessions, follow the chart at the end of this chapter.

Lectio on life is a powerful process because we intentionally bring the broken and confused places in our lives to God for healing. Sometimes painful or old memories can surface, and these may cause difficulty for the individual and the group. As in *lectio divina* with scripture, the basic principle is to trust in the healing and embracing presence of God in one's midst. However, in general, this group practice is not a substitute for those who are (or need to be) in crisis stages with psychotherapy.

Our incarnational principle encourages us to accept the wisdom of using the skilled resources available to help us heal both physical and emotional wounds. While prayer is always part of this healing, it is unnecessary to trust prayer as the single resource without supplementing it with those natural and human means through which grace ordinarily works. The psychotherapy now available is potentially an enormously helpful resource. Whenever we feel consistently depressed or confused or unable to cope with life issues, we may wish to consider exploring that resource. However, be aware that not all practitioners have been carefully trained or are licensed. If you decide to pursue this kind of help, seek a recommendation from someone whom you know and trust—either a friend whose therapist has proved helpful or a member of the clergy whose discernment you respect.

Persons may seek help for a variety of coping issues on a much broader continuum than was once the case. For example, many skilled helpers practice in the areas of marriage and family issues. At the other end of the scale are highly trained professionals who work with those suffering from severe psychic burdens such as multiple personality disorder, or schizophrenia. In particular, if and when the supportive intimacy of a *lectio* community seems to bring deeply troubling material to the surface, it is wise to consult a professional or pastoral advisor to determine whether therapeutic assistance could help.

As we gain strength through the prayerful support of loving Christians, sometimes old issues will begin to surface in *lectio* on life as an expression of our current readiness to work with these issues in therapy. Or we may already be in therapy and find prayer an essential support for the healing of memories, as in *lectio* we explore how God was actually present to us in ways we did not then realize. Always, the best support we can give one another is our ongoing love and care, and our entrusting of those we love to God who is doing for them more than we can ask or imagine. *Lectio* is designed to help us learn to do this for ourselves and one another in all times and places. May you too be blessed in this way.

Group *Lectio* on Life Process

The group *lectio* on life process includes these steps, slightly elaborated to assist the leader in practice.

Prepare.

1. **Hear the word.**

   Review recent life events and select a single incident for reflection

   • Give several minutes of silence for reviewing the hours and experiences of the last several days. Allow one event or situation to keep returning for attention.

   • Ask group members to state simply the approximate time of day when their chosen incident occurred.

2. **How is my life touched?**

   Review the incident mentally and emotionally as it happened, then be receptive to a phrase or image that seems to be given in relation to it:

   • Remind the group that "touched" refers to the touch of Christ.

   • Ask them to recreate the incident as it actually happened, remembering all they can about sights, sounds, etc. Allow one to two minutes for this undertaking.

   • Ask them to recreate the emotions of the incident: Where was the strongest energy or any major energy shift? Allow one to two minutes for this.

   • Ask them to set aside mentally all their musings after two or more minutes, and let their minds become receptive to a phrase or image from scripture or literature.

   • Remind them after two minutes to be aware that the given phrase or image is a blessing, a sign of Christ's presence in the incident. Ask group members to share only the phrase or image.*

3. **Is there an invitation here?**

   Offer the incident and your reflections back to God. Rest and be responsive to any invitation that might come.

   • Ask group members to bring back to memory their life incident and their image or phrase alongside it. Allow one minute to hold both in peace.

- Urge them to offer up everything to God mentally, to let it go for now.
- Ask them to be receptive to any invitation or encouragement that may come now to be or to do something in the next few days. Allow about one or two minutes of silence.
- Ask the members to share their invitation.*

4. **Pray for the person to the right.**
Afterward, the group members may share their thoughts and feelings about the process, if desired.

*Note: Anyone may pass at any time.

6 Our heritage

iverse sources commend the practice of *lectio* as a central tool of Christian faith. On the one hand are the sources of the past, rooted so deeply in the Christian heritage that it is likely Jesus himself practiced something like *lectio* in his earthly life. On the other hand are the sources of the present drawing us into the future, springing up in modern Christian practice wherever the church is at its liveliest and most relevant, so close to the emerging vitality of Christian growth that it seems to be a central contemporary manifestation of the spirit of God. This chapter describes some of these sources. The developed forms differ slightly, but both past and present sources clearly suggest what we have come to recognize as *lectio*: that slow, contemplative interaction with scripture that brings union with God and sinks into one's own heart as the ongoing, vibrant spring of new life.

Scripture Invites *Lectio*

The Scripture Passages

Scripture itself draws us to *lectio*. Although the poetry and wisdom literature in the

Psalms and Proverbs are especially rich in invitation to *lectio*, we can find encouragement throughout scripture, especially in the mature spiritual reflection of the community of faith. Periodic shifts in language and translation sometimes tend to obscure references to *lectio* in scripture, but let us look closely and consider the invitation that emerges.

> When I was a [child] with my father, tender, and my mother's favorite, he taught me, and said to me, "Let your heart hold fast my words; keep my commandments, and live."
>
> —Proverbs 4:3-4

Over and over in the psalms and proverbs we encounter this kind of invitation: My child, listen with the ear of your heart! The parents assume responsibility for giving the child not only the gift of life but the ongoing gift of knowing how to *live*. And the secret of this gift of life is that our heart "hold fast" to the words given. *Hold fast* and *keep* are terms that invite us to ponder, to reflect, to turn something over and over until it becomes part of our being. The offered words or commandments are not the arbitrary words of one human father but are rather the wisdom gathered by the whole community and generally expressed in the written tradition. These words are the words of God, the words of life.

At crucial points in the scripture, we find major actors practicing this exercise of reflective *lectio*. Abraham, David, and Mary are key examples. Take, for instance, the passage where God makes a covenant with Abraham. God promises that Abraham will be the ancestor of a multitude of nations, specifically through a child of his and Sarah's:

> Abraham fell on his face and laughed, and said to himself, "Can a child be born to a man who is a hundred years old?"
>
> —Genesis 17:17

The most literal translation is that Abraham "laughed in his heart," and the implication of the term *heart* is that he is taking this promise of God into his being, keeping it or turning it over in a reflective way, and thereby somehow cooperating with the transforming power of God. As we have seen, the human heart is the locus of our capacity for cooperating with God, the locus of our capacity for *lectio*. David, dedicating and crowning his son Solomon, summarizes the wisdom he has inherited from his community and manifested in his reign, in a consecrating prayer that embodies the *lectio* approach:

> I know, my God, that you search the heart, and take pleasure in uprightness. . . . now I have seen your people, who are present here, offering freely and joyously to you. O Lord, the God of Abraham [and Sarah], keep forever such purposes and thoughts in the hearts of your people, and direct their hearts toward you.
>
> —1 Chronicles 29:17-18

Again we notice these central scriptural terms: *keep* and *heart*. The terms in this prayer invite not merely a passive acceptance of God's purposes but rather an intention toward active engagement—meditating and internalizing the word of God.

To keep a thing is to care for it tenderly and to turn it frequently. God's law is to be savored like precious grains, root vegetables, or pots of honey that are stored away in some safe place, regularly examined and turned over so that they might be kept as ongoing sources of nurture. Everything comes from God, but we have an obligation to care for these gifts. A major means of care, especially for the most valued gift of the word, is to "store up" or "treasure."

In the New Testament, two central passages tell us that Mary, the mother of Jesus, kept something in her heart. Both of these passages occur in the second chapter of the Gospel of Luke. In the first, immediately after Jesus' birth, the shepherds visit Mary and Joseph. The shepherds tell their story and praise God. We read that Mary "treasured all these words and pondered them in her heart" (Luke 2:19). The word *treasure* comes from the same root word as *store*: It means keeping in a safe place that it ultimately may be used to strengthen and build up. Mary regularly returns to examine and turn over these words, carefully tending something precious that it may nourish her. She does this work in her heart.

Later on, when Jesus is twelve years old (the year he becomes a man), the holy family goes to Jerusalem for the festival of the Passover. This time Jesus stays behind and is lost to them; the parents must return to Jerusalem and undertake a long search, only to find him in the temple, which he calls "his Father's house." Again we read that "his mother treasured all these things in her heart" (Luke 2:51). Somehow in the midst of these perplexing yet important events of her life, Mary is using her heart to reflect. We might say she is doing *lectio*. And scripture suggests that her willingness to do this somehow enlarges her already mature capacity to respond to God and to continue to be a contributing part of God's purposes in the world.

As we become sensitive to the way *lectio* finds expression in human life, I think it is not difficult to read many of Jesus' sayings as the fruit of his own practice of something like *lectio*. Consider for example the answer Jesus gives to John the Baptist when John sends from prison to ask if Jesus is "the one to come." Jesus responds to this painful inquiry from his cousin and longtime friend in this way:

> Go and tell John what you hear and see: the blind receive their
> sight, the lame walk, the lepers are cleansed, the deaf hear, the
> dead are raised, the poor have the good news brought to them.
> And blessed is anyone who takes no offense at me.
>
> —Matthew 11:4-6

Will this answer comfort John? Yes, indeed! And why? It takes a little research to make the connection, but it is well worthwhile. Clearly Jesus is referring to passages in the Hebrew Scriptures—Isaiah 42:6-7 and 61:1—in his answer to John. He is evoking the image Isaiah presents of the Messiah as suffering servant. Of all those persons closely connected with Jesus in the Gospels, only John gives evidence that he shares this vision of the Messiah, the one to come, as suffering servant. Indeed, John has described his own ministry by referring to Isaiah's vision of the Messiah as suffering servant. He calls himself the "messenger, . . . the voice of one crying out in the wilderness: 'Prepare the way of the Lord'" (Mark 1:2-3). This language too comes from the prophet Isaiah (40:3). It appears near the passages Jesus quotes in his gentle and affirming answer to John. Is it too far-fetched to imagine Jesus and John as adolescents, poring together over their scriptures lectio style and finding in the words of Isaiah the ideas that later emerge in their individual and mutual sense of vocation?

The Words That Call Out

We have discovered two key words used in scripture to suggest what we have called *lectio*. These words commend a devotional, personalized, and imaginative approach as a means of taking inward and making personal the objective truth of the Word. Two code words of scripture that alert us to a practice of *lectio* are *heart* and *ponder* (or *keep*).

The heart is the locus of the person's capacity for this work of "keeping" things, which is the work of *lectio*. God's people are to give thanks with the heart (Ps. 138:1), to have courage in the heart (Ps. 27:3), to seek God with our whole heart (Ps. 119:2), and above all to have a clean heart (Ps. 51:10) and to be pure in heart (Ps. 73:1). Hannah's heart rejoices (1 Sam. 2:1), while David despairs in his heart (1 Sam. 21:12; 27:1). Things kept or turned over in the heart seem to evoke the transforming power of God, whether they are kept with delight or sorrow!

The Greek word *sumballo* ("ponder" in English) literally means "cast together" and suggests the major metaphor for *lectio* scriptural devotion, which is "keep." Precious goods were cast together or stored up, creating a treasure that was kept with care. In this sense, to "keep" (or to ponder) a thing means to set it aside with things that seem somehow similar to it, to turn all over in one's mind with some frequency, and to value it according to its ability to provide the nurture required for life.

Such a keeping involves a keen sense of stewardship of real, material things, while also acknowledging the sense in which they are *gift*. In just this sense, David "keeps" the sheep (1 Sam. 17:34), the people of Yahweh are to "keep" the covenant (Exod. 19:5), and the king himself is to "keep" the law (Deut. 17:14-20). Likewise, in the New Testament, Mary ponders, or keeps, these things in her heart (Luke 2:19, 51), allowing the mysterious interaction of event and of promise to enlarge her capacity for God.

Occasionally scripture evokes the *lectio* process with the word translated "meditate," as when a righteous person considers the law (Ps. 1:2). But the work of meditating and internalizing the Word of God is more often referred to with the more lively notion of keeping or pondering something in one's heart. Jesus calls us repeatedly to hear the word and keep it (see Luke 8:15; 11:28), meaning that we are to do with God's Word what we have called *lectio* as revealed in scripture and life, in order that the Word might abide in us. And the final book of the Bible, Revelation, begins and ends with a benediction for those who hear (the Word) and take to heart (that which is written in the scriptures). (See Rev. 1:3; 22:7, 9.)

Historical Usage and Development of *Lectio*

Hebrew Roots

The Hebrews used two main methods of scripture study. One was called *halakah*, meaning adherence to traditional rules of spiritual practice having a legal character (like the Ten Commandments). The other method was called *haggadah*, meaning a narrative, imaginative, and interactive interpretation of scripture. This second method involved stories, legends, and folklore in a devotional amplification of a biblical passage and development of a new thought based on it. This *haggadah* "is intended to bring heaven down to the congregation and also to lift them up to heaven."[4] It involves several levels of textual study—from the literal to the mysterious—via the free use of text to explore its inner meaning.

Frequently rabbinic commentaries on scripture employ this method. Haggadah was part of the devotional practice of Jews in Jesus' time. Faithful Jews internalized the words of the Torah, or Law, memorizing scripture in a process that involved repeating passages over and over softly with the lips until the words themselves gradually took up residence in the heart, there transforming the person's life. The human relation to God's law was one involving all aspects of one's being—mind, body, spirit. Thus the phrase "learning by heart" had a vastly different value in ancient Hebrew practice than the generally superficial meaning we currently assign it.

This Hebrew method is quite similar to the favorite method of Bible study in the first five Christian centuries, which is known as allegorical. This type of study involved literal, allegorical, moral, and eschatological (pertaining to the end of time) meanings. Christian monastic practice of *lectio divina* was an offshoot of the allegorical method, drawing on the older biblical and Hebrew sources as well.

Early Christian Centuries

Another important influence that shaped the early practice of *lectio* was the practice in Greek and Roman secular schools of *meditari*, which meant the active visualizing of something mentally in order to prepare for it before it happened. For example, in the fourth century John Cassian quotes Abbot Nesteros's words to a novice:

> If only you will transfer to the reading of and meditation upon the writings of the Spirit, the same diligence and earnestness which you say that you showed in those secular studies of yours. . . . it will come to pass that not only every purpose and thought of your heart, but also all the wanderings and rovings of your imagination will become to you a holy and unceasing pondering of the divine law. (Conference 14)

This passage suggests that even a secular approach to reading taught during these centuries involved a type of mental and emotional integration, which when applied to the particular words of Spirit-inspired scripture, can become a life-changing experience.

Yet the practice of *lectio* among Christians in the first centuries of Christianity was not primarily dependent upon secular sources. Indeed, as early as the middle of the third century we find Saint Cyprian of Carthage (d. 258), writing in his *Letter to Donatus*: "Be constant as well in prayer as in reading [*lectio*]; now speak with God, now let God speak with you, let Him instruct you in His precepts, let Him direct you."[5] We can see here the rhythm of activity and receptivity in prayer, or of life integrated with Word of God, that is so characteristic of the practice of *lectio*. We notice particularly that *lectio divina* was so common a practice in Cyprian's day that the word we now translate "reading" is equivalent for him to what we understand as *lectio*.

Lectio divina has been generally known as the Benedictine approach to scripture because it characterizes the Rule of Saint Benedict, which was written in the mid-sixth century and practiced in subsequent centuries of monasticism. In the chapter of Benedict's Rule on "Daily Manual Labor," he spelled out a pattern of community prayer, physical labor, and study (*lectio*) that formed a balanced set of activities for growth in all aspects of one's humanity. In this pattern, a person was to undertake *lectio* practice for about four hours each day!

Lectio was apparently so common a practice among Christians of his time that Benedict felt no need to describe it. However, *lectio* clearly involved those elements that have emerged as central throughout our discussion, even if not the specific format suggested in this text. *Lectio* was a slow, meditative reading of the Word balanced with periods of silent reflection. It was both active and receptive. Its principal orientation was toward a personal encounter with the living God that would cast light on present life issues, rather than the gathering of information. It was a way of taking the scripture to heart, of making its promises one's own in a transformed life.

In Benedict's time, the primary practice of *lectio* was personal, but *lectio* also formed a principal mode of attentive worship in the eight daily gatherings for common prayer that centered on the psalms. We find the root of this *lectio* process in Benedict's conviction that God calls out the invitation for deeper loving relationship to each Christian daily (RB Prologue 9-13). It is largely the Benedictine monastic tradition that has kept this precious treasure of *lectio* practice alive through the intervening centuries.

Perhaps we can understand more fully the practice of *lectio by the* monks, nuns, and oblates if we read a few paragraphs from the twelfth-century work of Guigo II, the Carthusian, called *The Ladder of Monks*. In this work, he attempts to provide a systematic analysis of the various stages or steps in the *lectio divina* process. Guigo wrote to his brother Gervase that while pondering "our spiritual work," it occurred to him that it might be considered in four stages. In lyrical prose, Guigo calls these four stages (1) reading (*lectio*), (2) meditation (*meditatio*), (3) prayer (*oratio*), and (4) contemplation (*contemplatio*). Obviously he uses all four of these terms rather specifically. He says,

> Reading seeks for the sweetness of a blessed life, meditation perceives it, prayer asks for it, contemplation tastes it. Reading, as it were, puts food whole into the mouth, meditation chews it and breaks it up, prayer extracts its flavor, contemplation is the sweetness itself which gladdens and refreshes. (Cist. St. #48, 68-69)[6]

For Guigo, the practice of *lectio* is the practice of a soul on fire with longing for the Loved One. It is a soul's response to the powerful attractiveness of the One for whom we were made. But *lectio* is not only the expression of longing on the human side; it is a means by which God's very self "breaks in upon the middle of our prayer, runs to meet us in all haste, . . . and restores our weary soul." It is a way in which God draws us into God's own life.

Reformation Experience

Words tend to change with worldviews, and we may find it difficult to trace *lectio* through the tumultuous period of the Reformation and the counter-Reformation. Although it is clear that some Reformers sought to do away with everything monastic, language shifts trace a careful keeping of the *lectio* mode of personal engagement with the living God in some of the Reformers' new language and in their personal practice with scripture.

For example, Martin Luther's "Instructions on How to Read the Holy Bible" suggest an approach congruent with *lectio* method in which Luther himself would have been spiritually formed. He asserts that the foundational principles of "reading" the Bible are first, humbly to implore God for enlightening grace, always bearing in mind that the Spirit-inspired word can only be understood by the Spirit presently in our midst; and second, bringing a mind free from ideas and a heart eager to know and do God's will. While Luther argues against the allegorical emphasis of then-catholic teaching by asserting the importance of never deviating from the literal meaning of the text, he also confesses awareness that the language of biblical authors often has special meaning that is hard to understand. For Luther, the key to understanding is always seeking to find Christ even and especially in the Old Testament passages, which is an allegorical approach.[7]

Clearly these elements parallel our mode of *lectio* practice. Our *lectio* method emphasizes the role of silence as a means of being open to the Spirit. It focuses on seeking Christ's presence as we ponder how the passage touches us. And it is oriented toward the heart as the responding center as we consider an invitation offered by the passage.

John Wesley, in his "Advice on Spiritual Reading," also suggests guidance remarkably parallel to the *lectio* process.

> Be sure to read, not cursorily or hastily, but leisurely, seriously, and with great attention; with proper pauses and intervals, and that you may allow time for the enlightenings of the divine grace. To this end, recollect, every now and then, what you have read, and consider how to reduce it to practice. . . . Read those passages over and over that more nearly concern yourself, and more closely affect your inclinations or practice. . . .
>
> . . . Select also any remarkable sayings or advices, and treasure them up in your memory; and these you may either draw forth in time of need . . . or make use of.[8]

Wesley urges slow reading with proper pauses for receptivity to the invitations of the Spirit, just as does our *lectio* process. He asks us to consider these invitations, such as they may be, in practical terms: how to reduce them to practice; or as we might say, how to integrate them as relevant touches to our daily lives. He too suggests the importance of the heart as the primary place of response, emphasizing that memorization is a means of receiving the scripture so that God's life may transform us from inside. Even in the tumultuous development of new denominations in the church, even across periods of dramatic shift in language and approaches to Christian experience, an emphasis survives on devotional presence with scripture for spiritual growth. And that emphasis strongly parallels the method presented here for group *lectio*.

Modern Developments

At one pivotal point in the New Testament, the Pharisees tell Jesus to make his followers be quiet, which is in effect a demand to shut down the people's growing faith in him as the Son of God. And he responds, "I tell you, if these were silent, the stones would shout out" (Luke 19:40). We have seen that the practice of *lectio divina* has been central to Christian devotional practice throughout the centuries. Yet because of its identification with monastic practice, it more or less went underground during the Reformation (in the sixteenth century) and has gradually fallen into disuse since the Enlightenment (in the eighteenth century). Since then, we have generally sought to approach the Bible with the mind rather than with the heart, and we have not known how to integrate what our mind tells us about scripture's gradual human evolution with what our hearts long for in terms of union with God. However, we can take comfort from Jesus' assurance that important things cannot be suppressed arbitrarily. As a powerful means of direct encounter with God that gives new hope for daily life, *lectio* is now bursting forth again in a groundswell of Christian experience, in a variety of places. The stones are shouting out the invitation to encounter God in scripture through this simple method.

New forms of *lectio* are blossoming forth in our own day in a number of Christian settings. Let's look at some of these.

In Africa
In South Africa, the Catholic bishops have established a religious education center called Lumko Institute that has developed an immensely popular Bible study method widely in use among new communities of Christians. Its model has seven steps that directly parallel the model offered in this book. These steps form the modern basis for the details of our *lectio* practice. These seven steps are as follows:

1. We invite the Lord.
2. We read the text.
3. We pick out words and meditate on them.
4. We let God speak to us in silence.
5. We share what we have heard in our hearts.
6. We discuss a sense of what we are called to do.
7. We pray together spontaneously.

This model is oriented explicitly to the life problems that members of the group experience. It intends to set God's Word in scripture alongside those problems to see what insights are revealed. And it is profoundly community-oriented: Life problems include not only personal ones but also those of the whole community, and the entire group is responsible to share certain tasks. The sessions always end with the explicit questions: *What does God want us to do?* and in response, *Who will do what and when?*

The Lumko method encourages a keen sense of expectancy that

God is living and active, directly concerned with the people's lives and specifically guiding and empowering certain communal actions.

In Latin America

In Latin America also, a new approach to Bible study has been developed. This approach, presented in a book called *The Gospel in Solentiname*, shares some aspects of *lectio* and includes some aspects not here. In this method, communal commentary on the scripture is substituted for the homily in the mass. The emphasis is not so much on what the gospel *should* mean, as on what it *does* mean to the illiterate and poverty-stricken faithful. It closely parallels *lectio* in its emphasis on a personal expectant listening, an eagerness to hear God's word in the scripture in a way that will give help for the vital struggles of daily life.

In the Solentiname approach, both the confidence in the Spirit's presence with the hearer, which enables reception of the Word, and the insistence that the living Word will always be in dialogue with concrete life issues, closely parallel our *lectio* practice. There is a deep conviction that Jesus lives and is present among those who call on him, mixed with awareness that the community of people is the *body* of Christ, and therefore given to one another for mutual comfort and care.

This strength of communal sharing also suggests the disparity between the Solentiname approach and the *lectio* model. The former focuses less on personal application and meaning and more on wider disorders of the social and political context. However, this broader social emphasis has given a personal sense of empowerment and value, which is the hoped-for outcome of the more personal emphasis in the *lectio* method presented here.

In the United States

The headquarters office of the Episcopal Church of the United States has picked up on this practice and has begun using it particularly in evangelism training. At a recent meeting, all the Episcopal bishops in the United States used this Bible reflection as part of their daily sessions. *Lectio* became the means of centering on their common faith in a time of considerable conflict on specific issues.

The United Methodist Church in its 1996 General Conference urged congregations to seek spiritual discernment in dealing with the complex issues of contemporary life. The delegates to the conference prepared themselves through participation in forty days of discernment prior to the conference.

The Roman Catholic Church in the United States has used a *lectio*-like practice extensively in their Rite of Christian Initiation of Adults, the catechumenate for adults. Their practice draws on the church's African and Latin American connections, as well as on a process offered by American Jesuits called *collatio*, or "shared meal." *Collatio* is actually a shared praying on scripture in a format very like the one we call *lectio*. That format also calls for three separate readings of the scripture with plenty of time for silence and a sequence of shared contributions. Sharing is brief yet personal and closes with spontaneous prayer. The Jesuits call the process *collatio* because it is a "collation" of everyone's contributions. Thus it brings forth a new creation centered in the word of scripture.

Summary

In this brief survey of modern developments in *lectio*, we see the tremendous hunger for an encounter with the sacred scriptures that is life-bringing. This hunger is evident among rich and poor, clergy and lay; among all denominations and across many continents. What is perhaps most amazing is the similarity among the methods chosen by many diverse movements of Christian people throughout the world as they turn to the Bible devotionally and for empowerment. The similarity of practice crosses not only the barriers of space but also those of time; we find many common elements among all the approaches.

I hope that the particular model of *lectio* offered here will aid the already strong movement of God's people who are reading God's Word, inspired by God's spirit.

Epilogue
Longing Transformed

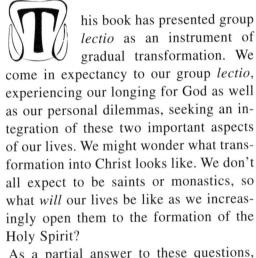 his book has presented group *lectio* as an instrument of gradual transformation. We come in expectancy to our group *lectio*, experiencing our longing for God as well as our personal dilemmas, seeking an integration of these two important aspects of our lives. We might wonder what transformation into Christ looks like. We don't all expect to be saints or monastics, so what *will* our lives be like as we increasingly open them to the formation of the Holy Spirit?

As a partial answer to these questions, this chapter provides an imaginary gathering of our sample *lectio* group after they have been meeting for a little over a year. The group has already had its annual evaluation meeting, and all six have decided they would like to continue together in the same format for another year. This meeting is about a month later.

Example

The group has gathered and settled. Ann is the leader tonight, and she has selected Hosea 2:14-15a for the scripture. She makes sure the chairs are in a circle and takes some time to connect by word or touch with each member present before the group convenes. She has been praying all week and is somewhat nervous about leading, but she feels confident in this small group of supportive friendship and is willing to see what happens.

When everyone is seated, she says, "I always like the first few minutes of our meetings best—when I come in a little tense and anxious, and we all just take a few minutes to be together and relax and remember Jesus is here. So let's do that now for a few minutes—remembering to check our posture and our breathing and to soak up the loving care we all bring for one another in this moment." There is a little shuffling, and then silence for a few minutes.

Ann says, "Listen now to the scripture. I'll read it twice; first for you to hear it overall and then again more slowly for you each to hear your own special word. The passage is from Hosea 2:

Therefore, I will now allure her, and bring her into the wilderness, and speak tenderly to her. From there I will give her her vineyards, and will make the Valley of Achor a door of hope. There she shall respond as in the days of her youth.

Ann reads the scripture again more slowly for each person to sense a word or phrase that speaks to his or her need.

After about a minute's silence, Ann says, "Okay, now let's each just say the word or phrase from the passage that seems to speak to us. Mine is 'a door of hope.'"

Jim responds, "In the days of youth."
Charles says, "Into the wilderness."
Mary voices, "Her youth."
Sharon says, "Tenderly."
Bill states, "Allure."

Ann nods in acknowledgment and then asks Jim to read the passage again, handing him the Bible. She says, "This time as we hear the scripture, we are listening with the question in mind: "How is my life touched?' We remember that touch may be physical, or it just may be a connection we sense. Listen now and in the silence after the reading."

Jim reads the passage, and Ann consults her watch so she will know when two minutes have elapsed. Then she closes her own eyes in meditation. At the end of two minutes, she speaks, "We can share now how we sense our lives touched. Just a sentence or two."

After a few seconds, Charles begins, "I'm thinking about what the wilderness is for me. I used to think of it as a barren place, but since I've been backpacking regularly in the desert, I've come to appreciate its subtle charms. I feel there is a parallel somehow in my life with its mix of barrenness and unexpected blossoming."

Mary adds, "My youth . . . I have a sense of such carefree lightness . . . I miss it."

There is a silence. Then Jim says, "Youth means something different for me, I think. When I was a kid, I was very serious. I get a picture of this little owl with glasses on! That was me." He laughs ruefully.

Bill says, "You know, I almost feel Jesus tempting me, if you can say that. It's like he's pulling on my heart, saying 'love me'—almost erotically. Wow, it's like I desire to be with him more than anything!" He looks embarrassed.

Sharon responds, "I see our little daughter with the neighbor's big old dog. He always treats her with such infinite patience and care. It's almost as if he knows his own great strength. Even when she accidentally hurts him, he never strikes out at her."

Ann says, "I hear music; it seems to come from somewhere far off—both vocal and instrumental, with haunting beauty. And even though it is far away, it is wrapping around me and enfolding me in delight. It's almost like I live in it, just as a fish lives in water all around." She pauses, then says, "All right, let's hear the passage for the last time." She passes the Bible to Mary and states " This time we'll listen especially for an invitation that seems to be here for each of us: something to be or do within the next few days or week."

Mary reads the passage again, and Ann lets three minutes elapse this time before speaking, "Now we may share. This time we can speak a bit more if we wish, and we are sharing what, if any, invitation seemed to come to us from the passage for our lives right now. Anyone is welcome to pass if you wish. Remember to pay special attention to the one sharing on your right."

Mary says, "As I myself read the passage, I heard something I had not heard before. It is not just a recalling of the days of my youth with nostalgia; something else is happening here. It is God's loving and giving and bringing into being something *for me*—something as lovely as youth but even better. It is not just fixing something broken but some new wholeness that goes beyond what was possible then. I think the invitation for me is to relax and let God do things in me that I can't do for myself. . . . Uh, specifically, I feel I'm being invited to take a couple of hours during this week to do something just for the pure pleasure of it! I don't necessarily have to fight for pleasure; maybe I can just flow with it when it's given!"

Bill grins at her. "Amen to that! I have this funny and kind of unsettling impression that I'm being invited to enjoy and honor my *desires*! That sounds weird, but what I mean is that, well, . . . I keep going back to that question Jesus asked me in our first meeting: 'What do you want?' And every time I answer it, it's as if I go deeper and deeper inside myself. What I really want is to be with Jesus all the time. Gosh, words are so awkward!

"Anyway, the impression I have is that Jesus himself puts that desire deep in my heart and is almost alluring me to let him be first in my life. And as I let that happen, there's kind of a difference in everything. I'm enjoying Mary and the kids more, but I'm less demanding of them. I'm taking a day off from work now and then, and I'm actually finding that in being less compulsive about work in general, I'm enjoying it more. Not that all is roses, by any means—the economy is still rotten; and my boss is still a stickler for detail, but you know—it's fun now! I guess my invitation is to keep having fun. Wow, that sure doesn't sound like a spiritual discipline, does it? " He grins again and shakes his head.

Charles says, "That's sort of what I'm feeling too, Bill, but also a little different. Like Jim, I've always been a kind of serious guy, and I'm always trying so hard to figure things out. But you know, just when I begin to think I've got a handle on something, they change the rules on me. I've been driving myself crazy trying to keep on top of everything; for example, the way I've been glued to public television these last few days, you'd think they couldn't run the Congress without me! So anyway, it's been real good for me to begin paying more attention to the physical world and to my body—like camping in the desert. I've been noticing things I never saw before, and for me that desert really is a place of hope. I watch the seasons change and the tiny blossoms appear given the least little encouragement of water or sunshine, and there's a sense of continuity and peacefulness that's just great. I feel real good about myself—I've even lost thirty pounds! My invitation is just to keep at these simple things that I know are so good for me, even for my soul!"

Sharon says, "For me those simple physical things—the flowers in the meadow, the hot soapy dishwater, the children and animals always have been important, but it's almost as if they are deepening in importance now. My main work right now seems to be mainly to deal seriously with my depression and to face the truth of my childhood abuse. And sometimes that is overwhelming in its pain and its power. But often when it seems just too much, a sunbeam will glance through the kitchen window, almost like the finger of God tenderly plucking on the strings of my heart, and I feel the sudden bittersweet delight of simply being alive! So for me the invitation is to trust in the tenderness, to believe that God is like the neighbor's dog—improbable as that sounds—and the power is always tempered by loving care for me."

There is another pause, and then Jim says, "On this last reading, I heard a new word that had not struck me before, and that was *vineyards*. I have always been particularly attracted to the image of Israel as God's vineyard or God's grapevine, and for years I have appreciated the historical metaphor of the grapevine in Psalm 80. You remember that in that psalm, Israel is crying out to God, asking why he allows the vine (themselves) to be trampled underfoot, when he previously planted them and cared for them so tenderly. It is an impressive feat for the psalmist and prophets to come up with the understanding that their country was suffering so much war and looting because the people had defaulted on their covenant with God and had depended on their own strength. . . . "

Jim glances over at Ann, clears his throat, is silent for a moment. Then he says, "What I am trying to say is that when I was a youngster, I always felt that I was God's favorite, that I was specially chosen. And that's not necessarily a bad thing; it's just that I started feeling so responsible, to be singled out like that and given so many blessings. And I began to think it was my job to set everyone on the right track and to fix everything. And this ongoing problem with Ann's mom has just set me on my tail. That woman baffles me; she just won't listen to reason. She's irrational, and nothing that I can do makes the slightest impact on her. Meanwhile, she's wrecking our lives! But it's the oddest thing: Somehow the fact that I couldn't fix it for Ann—or for me—has made me realize all over again, like I haven't felt since I was a kid, how very much I need God. And I've prayed like I haven't prayed for years, really *needing* God's help. And it's not that everything has miraculously cleared up, though it is a little better. But I feel a whole lot better. Thanks to you all I know I have help, and that's good. So I need to just keep asking for help."

There is a warmly shared silence. At last Ann says, "For me these days, there is hope. Jesus still seems far away, but through you friends and our time together, I suspect that he is near too. My invitation is just to hold on to that hope—or maybe even better, to keep opening that door just a little bit more whenever I can. Dear friends, let's pray together."

All bow their heads, and Ann takes Jim's hand. "Jesus," Ann

prays, "thank you for Jim. I pray that you will fill all his needs. Amen." All echo amen.

Mary prays for Ann, "Mother God, tenderly take our friend Ann into your embrace in a way that she has never known and let her be nourished and strengthened in your bosom. Amen." All say amen.

Charles prays for Mary, "God, you have given Mary the gift of bringing to all around her so much joy; do give her those special couple of hours with you this week and let her relax into the joy you would give her. Amen." All say amen.

Sharon prays for Charles, "Our God, be with my husband, who is so often aware of his own barrenness, even when others of us see mainly his wonderful blossoms. Thank you for helping us to share this love of nature. Amen." All say amen.

Bill prays for Sharon, "Lord, we grieve that our sister has to suffer so much pain, but we trust that every day you are bringing her some healing. Let her continue to see your tender care each day in some gift of the day. Amen." All say amen.

Jim prays for Bill, "Father, thank you for reaching into Bill's heart and letting him know that you gave your Son because you love him and the world so much. I pray you will keep him in the happiness of knowing that deep in his being. Amen." All say amen.

Ann says, "Let's all say the Lord's Prayer together by way of a closing blessing." And they do.

In this example we see that transformation into Christ looks perfectly ordinary. In Christ, we do not stop being the persons we are; we do not float around like angels. We bring the fullness of our personality to our prayer, and there we discover an increasing richness of life previously only glimpsed. Problems do not disappear, but we have a better perspective on them; and we can value and receive the genuine help available to handle them. There is a sense of greater balance and wholeness in our lives and an awareness that pain and joy are both part of the gift of being human.

Our thirst for a deeper life in God does not diminish and actually may increase. But our thirst is matched by a sense that we are also receiving regular and satisfying spiritual refreshment and strength for the journey. We feel part of a whole people of God, living and dead, in whose support we receive strength. God's life in us becomes a practical resource, accessible and fruitful in the living of our ordinary lives. The Word in us prospers and so do we. God bless the longing of every heart, as we share this journey of spiritual growth through praying scripture together.

Appendix
I Seek Thee, Lord
Praying Scripture Alone

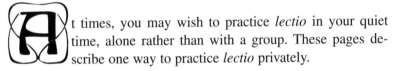t times, you may wish to practice *lectio* in your quiet time, alone rather than with a group. These pages describe one way to practice *lectio* privately.

Select the passage.

First, select the passage you will use and mark your place in scripture. Remember that *lectio* requires a short passage—possibly only two or three verses but no more than ten at a time. If you wish to practice *lectio* while reading a whole book of scripture, say the Gospel of Mark, it is important not to rush and not to measure your practice by the number of verses to be covered each day. Rather, allocate the amount of time you will give to your daily practice, and proceed through only as many verses as you can at the leisurely pace of *lectio*. If it takes two years to "finish" the one Gospel, it does you no harm; indeed, you may harvest great fruits.

Take time to be fully present.

Second, set aside your Bible and take some time to quiet down and reach the place of interior silence in your heart. Breathe and release tension. Let preoccupations go out with your breath. Breathe in God's very presence. Breathe in confidence and security and peace. Take plenty of time here. As your mind starts to wander, *gently* return your attention to your breathing. Wait until you sense your body is quieted before you open your eyes and pick up your Bible.

Receive your word or phrase.

Read the passage you have selected slowly and aloud. Read it again even more slowly. Linger over each word and be receptive to whatever claims your interest. Some word or phrase may draw your attention; some expression may repel you. Wherever you find yourself responding with real energy, whether positive or negative energy, stop there.

Close your eyes again, and repeat over and over the word or phrase that has sought your attention, softly but aloud. For now, don't think about it or do anything with it, just allow your lips to feel the word and your ears to hear it, and let it become one with the rhythm of your breath. Engage your body with the scripture. When the word is firmly established in your senses, turn your thoughts to it.

Think about the word or phrase.

Read the same passage of scripture again aloud. Let your mind interact with the word or phrase now. Think about what the word or phrase is, and how this passage uses it. What do you think it means? Consider all you know about this word or phrase, both naturally and spiritually. For example, suppose the phrase that you are praying today is "five loaves" from Mark 6:38-44. You might think about bread: how it is made and what a nourishing staple food it is. You might consider how often scripture uses bread to symbolize God's presence and power among us. Perhaps you ponder why all the Gospels record this particular event and wonder that it seems a sort of foretaste of the Last Supper. Many thoughts are brought into consideration at this time; let your mind be fully engaged with the scripture.

Explore feelings evoked by the word or phrase.

Perhaps you want to read the same passage aloud again. Now respond with your feelings about what you have read. Let your imagination freely engage the word or phrase given to you and allow your memory and your dreams to play here too. Possibly you recall a time when you tried making bread and didn't use enough flour in the kneading process, so your fingers swelled up with layers of sticky, wet dough. Or maybe you find yourself drawn into the biblical scene itself, and you wonder if you would have dared to offer five small loaves to Jesus to feed such a crowd. Do you long for the simple faith that sees abundance where others see only need? At this time, you will find yourself associating the passage with current themes in your own life: What kind of nourishment do you need? How are you invited to serve others with what seems like limited resources? What has Jesus amazingly multiplied in you?

Release and offer all to God.

When your thoughts and feelings have taken you as far as they can, and you find yourself beginning to go over the same ground, let them go. As much as possible for you today, release everything that you have been thinking and feeling and offer it all to God. You may have gained rich insight, or you may feel even more "stuck" than you did before you began. In whatever state you find yourself at this time, let it go; give it to God. You may wish to express your release physically by giving a big sigh or by opening your hands or by otherwise confirming with your body what you seek to express with your deepest will.

Give everything to God right now, knowing that God may return it to you later but that in God's hands it will be transformed and made sacred. However, you may find that you are not able to release *everything* to God yet; if so, give whatever you can right now. Sometimes it is better to offer our life to God bit by bit rather than all at once; we are less likely to be able to leave *everything* with God. One woman said she had offered her "bag of garbage" at the altar hundreds of times, but she had never yet seen herself leaving the altar empty-handed; she always took the garbage bag back with her! So for now, give what you can—not what you can't.

Whatever you can release to God now, do so and let yourself experience the relief. Know the lighter burden, the rest and peace that can come from letting God handle everything for a few moments. As much as possible, sit in silence without comment, safe and at ease, wholly in the present moment.

Receive what is offered.

As you wait on God, you may find that a sort of invitation or insight seems to emerge. Without force or insistence, your receptive openness to the Holy One may allow you to sense something that you feel encouraged to be or do in response to your *lectio* today. It may be a minor thing, perhaps simply a willingness to live further into a certain tension in your life without forcing a decision. Or perhaps you experience a new vitality for a long-postponed task that you must do. You may feel a grudge less strongly or be overwhelmed with thankfulness for an old and reliable friendship. Allow your deep will to be drawn into greater harmony with God's. If or when you feel reasonably certain of the next best step, commit yourself to it.

It is appropriate to leave your *lectio* with a word or phrase that you will carry with you as a sort of divine bouquet to sniff at lovingly throughout that day or the one that follows, reminding you of God's fidelity. You may offer verbal thanks to God before closing.

When you are ready, gently and slowly open your eyes, wiggle your fingers and toes, and gradually return. You may wish to journal for a few moments on your experience. If you have time, you may continue your *lectio* by repeating this process with the next few verses of scripture before you. Or you may simply return refreshed to whatever awaits you.

Any listing is merely a helpful aid to understand the integral elements of the whole, and there is nothing sacred about the sequence of personal *lectio* described here. However, it may help to practice it in this order for a time, until the natural rhythms of your spirit take its place.

Personal *Lectio*

1. Select the passage.
2. Takc time to be fully present.
3. Receive your word or phrase.
4. Think about the word.
5. Explore feelings evoked by the word or phrase.
6. Release and offer all to God.
7. Receive what is offered.

Notes

1. The primary source for *lectio divina* is monastic experience, especially as required by the Rule of Saint Benedict of Nursia, who makes *lectio* a substantial element in each day's schedule. He wrote the Rule in the mid-sixth century, and it has formed the basis for Christian monastic practice since then. See *The Rule of Saint Benedict in Latin and English with Notes*, Timothy Fry, Senior Editor and Translator, (Collegeville, MN: The Liturgical Press, 1981) or my own commentary on the Rule called *Preferring Christ*, which has a translation of the Rule by Luke Dysinger (Trabuco Canyon, CA: Source Books, 1991).

2. Carl Rogers, *On Becoming a Person* (Boston: Houghton Mifflin/Sentry), 331–32.

3. C. S. Lewis, *Letters to Malcolm: Chiefly on Prayer* (London: Fontana Books, 1966), 77.

4. See Isador Singer, ed., *The Jewish Encyclopedia*, vols. VI and VIII, especially the article on "Midrash Haggadah"(New York: Funk and Wagnalls, 1904), quoted from Zunz, GV, 349.

5. From *The Ante-Nicene Fathers*, vol. V (Grand Rapids, MI: Wm. B. Eerdmans, 1956), 279–80.

6. From *The Ladder of Monks* (Kalamazoo, MI: Cistercian Publications, 1981), 68–69.

7. T. A. Readwin, ed., *The Prefaces to the Early Editions of Martin Luther's Bible*, (London: Hatchard and Co., 1863).6.

8. Frank Whaling, ed., *John and Charles Wesley: Selected Writings* (New York: Paulist Press; 1981), 88–89.

Additional Resources

You may wish to consult this list of books for additional information on the practice of *lectio divina* and related group dynamics topics:

De Mello, Anthony. *Sadhana: A Way to God.* New York: Doubleday/Image Books, 1984. Especially Exercise 33.

Dysinger, Luke. "Accepting the Embrace of God: The Ancient Art of '*Lectio Divina*,'" *The Valyermo Benedictine*: Vol. 1: No.1, 33–43.

Hall, Thelma. *Too Deep for Words: Rediscovering Lectio Divina.* Mahwah, NJ: Paulist Press, 1988.

Hestenes, Roberta. *Using the Bible in Groups.* Louisville, KY: Westminster John Knox, 1985.

Leclerq, Jean. *The Love of Learning and the Desire for God*, 3rd edition. New York: Fordham University Press, 1982. Especially Part One, "The Formation of Monastic Culture": Chapter one, "The Conversion of St. Benedict."

Michael, Chester P. and Marie C. Norrisey. *Prayer and Temperament: Different Prayer Forms for Different Personality Types.* Charlottesville, VA: The Open Door, Inc., 1991, especially pages 31–45.

Mulholland, M. Robert. *Shaped by the Word: The Power of Scripture in Spiritual Formation.* Nashville, TN: The Upper Room, 1985.

Muto, Susan A. *A Practical Guide to Spiritual Reading.* Petersham, MA: St. Bede's Publications, 1994.

Panimolle, Salvatore, ed. *Like the Deer That Yearns: Listening to the Word and Prayer.* Petersham, MA: St. Bede's Publications, 1996.

Pennington, M. Basil. *Monastic Life: A Short History of Monasticism and Its Spirit.* Petersham, MA: St. Bede's Publications, 1989.

_____. *Light from the Cloister: Monastic Spirituality for Lay People.* New York: Paulist Press, 1991. Especially the chapter on "Listening."

Saint Benedict, the Rule of, in Latin and English with Notes, edited by Timothy Fry et al. Collegeville, MN: The Liturgical Press, 1981. Especially chapter 6: "The Role and Interpretation of Scripture in the Rule of St. Benedict."

Smith, Martin. *The Word Is Very Near You: A Guide to Praying with Scripture.* Boston: Cowley Publications, 1989.

Vest, Norvene. *No Moment Too Small: Rhythms of Silence, Prayer, and Holy Reading.* Boston: Cowley Publications, 1994. Especially chapter 2 on "Holy Reading."

Wiederkehr, Macrina. *A Tree Full of Angels: Seeing the Holy in the Ordinary.* San Francisco: HarperSanFrancisco, 1995.